# THE WORKS 5

*Paul Cookson*

Paul has compiled and edited over forty books of poetry and is probably one of the most famous poets you have never heard of. He has been writing poetry for over thirty years and published his first collection when he was eighteen. It wasn't very good but it was a start. After college he taught full-time for five years before realizing that poetry could be a job as well as a hobby. For over sixteen years he has worked as a poet in schools, performing his work and leading workshops. Sometimes he does this with David Harmer as *Spill the Beans*. Paul is an avid football fan and supports Everton. He is also the Poet-in-Residence at the National Football Museum in Preston.

Paul is married to Sally and they have two children – Sam and Daisy.

For more information you can visit Paul's website:
www.paulcooksonpoet.co.uk

D0494652

*Also available from Macmillan*

The Works
Every kind of poem
you will ever need for the Literacy Hour
*Chosen by Paul Cookson*

The Works 2
Poems on every subject
and for every occasion
*Chosen by Brian Moses and Pie Corbett*

The Works 3
A Poet a Week
*Chosen by Paul Cookson*

The Works 4
Every kind of poem
on every topic that you will
ever need for the Literacy Hour
*Chosen by Pie Corbett and Gaby Morgan*

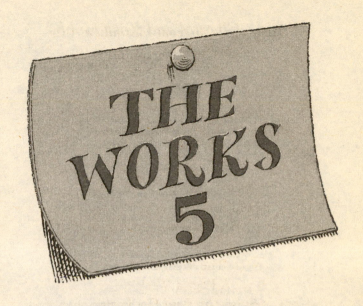

Every kind of poem, from an alphabet of poets,

that you will ever need for the Literacy Hour

# Chosen by Paul Cookson

MACMILLAN CHILDREN'S BOOKS

*To Andy, Chantal and Rosa Hobbs*

First published 2006 by Macmillan Children's Books
a division of Macmillan Publishers Limited
20 New Wharf Road, London N1 9RR
Basingstoke and Oxford
www.panmacmillan.com

Associated companies throughout the world

ISBN-13: 978-0330-39870-1
ISBN-10: 0-330-39870-9

1 3 5 7 9 8 6 4 2

A CIP catalogue record for this book is available from
the British Library.

Typeset by Intype Libra Ltd
Printed and bound in Great Britain by Mackays of Chatham plc, Kent

# Contents

## A is for . . .

## B is for . . .

# Contents

## C is for . . .

# Contents

## D is for . . .

# Contents

## E is for . . .

## F is for . . .

# Contents

## G is for . . .

## H is for . . .

# Contents

## I is for . . .

## J is for . . .

## K is for . . .

# Contents

## L is for . . .

## M is for . . .

# Contents

## N is for . . .

# Contents

## O is for . . .

## P is for . . .

# Contents

## Q is for . . .

## R is for . . .

## S is for . . .

# Contents

## T is for . . .

# Contents

## U is for . . .

## V is for . . .

## W is for . . .

# Contents

# Introduction

Hello and welcome to An Alphabet of Poets.

This book is just that – an alphabet of poets – an A–Z of poets both old and new. There will be poets you have heard of and poets you haven't, poets who are new, poets who are old and poets who are very, very old.

Trying to find poets for every letter of the alphabet was challenging – particularly with some of the letters! But – thanks to some creative investigation – we got there in the end, and while it may not be *the* definitive collection of poets it is certainly a definitive collection of some of the most important poets throughout the years.

However, what *is* important is not the poets themselves but the poems. There will be poems here that will make you smile and make you laugh while others may make you sit and think quietly. What is certain is that there is something for everyone. No one can leave this book without finding a poem and a poet that they like, hopefully someone new to them.

If there's one good thing about being an editor then it's that you can include all your favourite poets – and I have!

So dip in, explore this book of letters and find your own favourites.

*Paul Cookson*

# *A is for . . .*

## The Older the Violin the Sweeter the Tune

Me Granny old
Me Granny wise
stories shine like a moon
from inside she eyes.

Me Granny can dance
Me Granny can sing
but she can't play violin.

Yet she always saying,
'Dih older dih violin
de sweeter de tune.'

Me Granny must be wiser
than the man inside the moon.

*John Agard*

## Friendly Matches

In friendly matches
Players exchange pleasantries
Hallo, George!
How's the Missus?
Admire opponents' kit
Smart shirt, Bert!
Sympathize with linesmen
Difficult decision, there.
And share their half-time oranges.

In friendly matches
Players apologize for heavy tackles
How clumsy of me.
And offer assistance with throw-ins
Allow us to help you with that heavy ball.

In friendly matches
Players and substitutes alike
Speak well of referees
First-rate official
Sound knowledge of the game
Excellent eyesight!

In friendly matches
Players celebrate opposing players' birthdays
With corner-flag candles
On pitch-shaped cakes.

In friendly matches
Players take it in turns
No, no, please, after *you*

to score.

*Allan Ahlberg*

## Portrait of a Dragon

If I were an artist
I'd paint the portrait
of a dragon.

To do a proper job
I'd borrow colours
from the world.

For his back I'd
need a mountain range,
all misty blue.

For spikes I'd use
dark fir trees pointing
to the sky.

For overlapping scales
I'd squeeze dye from
bright anemones.

5

I'd gild his claws
like shining swords
  with starlight.

His tail would be
a river, silver
  in the sun.

For his head, the
secret green of forests
  and deep seas,

and his eyes would
glow like embers in
  a tinker's fire.

But I'd keep the best
till last. For his
  hot breath

I'd use all reds and
yellows – crocus, saffron,
  peony, poppy,

geranium, cyclamen, rose –
and fierce orange flames
  from a marigold.

*Moira Andrew*

## Life Doesn't Frighten Me

Shadows on the wall
Noises down the hall
Life doesn't frighten me at all
Bad dogs barking loud
Big ghosts in a cloud
Life doesn't frighten me at all.

Mean old Mother Goose
Lions on the loose
They don't frighten me at all
Dragons breathing flame
On my counterpane
That doesn't frighten me at all.

I go boo
Make them shoo
I make fun
'Way them run
I won't cry
So they fly
I just smile
They go wild
Life doesn't frighten me at all.

Tough guys in a fight
All alone at night
Life doesn't frighten me at all.
Panthers in the park
Strangers in the dark
No, they don't frighten me at all.

That new classroom where
Boys all pull my hair
(Kissy little girls
With their hair in curls)
They don't frighten me at all.

Don't show me frogs and snakes
And listen for my screams,
If I'm afraid at all
It's only in my dreams.

I've got a magic charm
That I keep up my sleeve,
I can walk the ocean floor
And never have to breathe.

Life doesn't frighten me at all
Not at all
Not at all
Life doesn't frighten me at all.

*Maya Angelou*

## Holiday Weather
### Poem to read at breakfast

I'm sorry to have to inform you,
The sun has been cancelled today.
Would customers dressed in bikinis,
Put their overcoats on straightaway.

You may wipe off sun-cream at your leisure,
Fling your old straw hat far out to sea,
Fold the deckchairs and tell the landlady
You'll be wanting lamb hotpot for tea.

Bank holidays aren't just for people,
The sun's worked non-stop since July,
Now he fancies a day with his feet up
So hurry indoors where it's dry.

*Petonelle Archer*

## *The Catch*

Forget
the long, smouldering
afternoon. It is

this moment
when the ball scoots
off the edge

of the bat; upwards,
backwards, falling
seemingly

beyond him
yet he reaches
and picks it

out
of its loop
like

an apple
from a branch,
the first of the season.

*Simon Armitage*

## Night Mail

This is the night mail crossing the border,
Bringing the cheque and the postal order,
Letters for the rich, letters for the poor,
The shop at the corner and the girl next door.
Pulling up Beattock, a steady climb –
The gradient's against her, but she's on time.

Past cotton grass and moorland boulder
Shovelling white steam over her shoulder,
Snorting noisily as she passes
Silent miles of wind-bent grasses.
Birds turn their heads as she approaches,
Stare from the bushes at her blank-faced coaches.
Sheepdogs cannot turn her course,
They slumber on with paws across.
In the farm she passes no one wakes,
But the jug in the bedroom gently shakes.

Dawn freshens, the climb is done
Down towards Glasgow she descends
Towards the steam tugs yelping down the glade of cranes,
Towards the fields of apparatus, the furnaces
Set on the dark plain like gigantic chessmen.
All Scotland waits for her:
In the dark glens, beside the pale-green lochs
Men long for news.

Letters of thanks, letters from banks,
Letters of joy from girl and boy,
Receipted bills and invitations
To inspect new stock or visit relations,
And applications for situations
And timid lovers' declarations
And gossip, gossip from all the nations,
News circumstantial, news financial.
Letters with holiday snaps to enlarge in,
Letters with faces scrawled in the margin,
Letters from uncles, cousins and aunts,
Letters to Scotland from the South of France,
Letters of condolence to Highlands and Lowlands,
Notes from overseas to Hebrides –
Written on paper of every hue,
The pink, the violet, the white and the blue,
The chatty, the catty, the boring, adoring,
The cold and official and the heart's outpouring,
Clever, stupid, short and long,
The typed and the printed and the spelt all wrong.
Thousands are still asleep
Dreaming of terrifying monsters,
Of a friendly tea beside the band at Cranston's or
   Crawford's:
Asleep in working Glasgow, asleep in well-set Edinburgh,
Asleep in granite Aberdeen.
They continue their dreams;
But shall wake soon and long for letters,

And none will hear the postman's knock
Without a quickening of the heart,
For who can hear and feel himself forgotten?

*W. H. Auden*

## Oh, I Wish I'd Looked After Me Teeth

Oh, I wish I'd looked after me teeth,
   And spotted the perils beneath
All the toffees I chewed,
   And the sweet sticky food.
Oh, I wish I'd looked after me teeth.

I wish I'd been that much more willin'
   When I had more tooth there than fillin'
To give up gobstoppers,
   From respect to me choppers,
And to buy something else with me shillin'.

When I think of the lollies I licked
   And the liquorice allsorts I picked,
Sherbet dabs, big and little,
   All that hard peanut brittle,
My conscience gets horribly pricked.

My mother, she told me no end,
   'If you got a tooth, you got a friend.'
I was young then, and careless,
   My toothbrush was hairless,
I never had much time to spend.

Oh I showed them the toothpaste all right,
   I flashed it about late at night,
But up-and-down brushin'
   And pokin' and fussin'
Didn't seem worth the time – I could bite!

If I'd known I was paving the way
   To cavities, caps and decay,
The murder of fillin's,
   Injections and drillin's,
I'd have thrown all me sherbet away.

So I lay in the old dentist's chair,
   And I gaze up his nose in despair,
And his drill it do whine
   In these molars of mine.
'Two amalgam,' he'll say, 'for in there.'

How I laughed at my mother's false teeth,
   As they foamed in the waters beneath.
But now comes the reckonin'
   It's *me* they are beckonin'
Oh, I *wish* I'd looked after me teeth.

*Pam Ayres*

# B is for . . .

## The Feeling of Snow
## Before the Snow Itself Falls

It's not just the sharp coldness
that's there in the air,
or the sight of your own breath,
when the weather turns
and you're walking far from town;
but still suddenly
you know it's going to snow –

and you look upwards
where, just before the snow comes,
the grey sky now shines
with the browns of winter earth,
and copper-tinged clouds
prepare to send their whiteness
over everything.

It's as if you can taste it
even from the ground:
the snow waiting in the clouds.
And you taste it still
as the first flakes flutter down:
the feeling of snow
before the snow itself falls.

*David Bateman*

## The Vulture

The Vulture eats between his meals,
    And that's the reason why
He very, very rarely feels
    As well as you or I.
His eye is dull, his head is bald,
    His neck is growing thinner.
Oh, what a lesson for us all
    To only eat at dinner.

*Hilaire Belloc*

## Early to Bed Early to Rise

The early bird catches the worm;
He is early to bed and to rise.
    For him worms equal wealth
    And in matters of health
Such habits as these are wise.
    But the worm, poor dull beast,
    (Who takes part in this feast)
Does not know the sayings of old.
    With nocturnal wandering
    His life he is squandering
(What a pity he never was told).
    If only they'd said

About early to bed,
Given warning re going to bed late,
He'd have been tucked away
At the breaking of day
And not on some bird's breakfast plate.

*Catherine Benson*

## Contentment

I'm glad the sky is painted blue:
And the earth is painted green;
And such a lot of nice fresh air
All sandwiched in between.

*E. Clerihew Bentley*

## Not Sharing

My sister stays on her new bicycle.
It has parts shining like silver.
The wheel tyres are black.
The seat leather is dark brown.
My sister cleans her bicycle minutely.
She rides it round and round our garden.
She rides it up and down our street.

19

My sister is never tired
of her new bicycle. If she was, ever,
I might just get a ride on it.

*James Berry*

## A Bay in Anglesey

The sleepy sound of a tea-time tide
Slaps at the rocks the sun has dried,

Too lazy, almost, to sink and lift
Round low peninsulas pink with thrift.

The water, enlarging shells and sand,
Grows greener emerald out from land

And brown over shadowy shelves below
The waving forests of seaweed show.

Here at my feet in the short cliff grass
Are shells, dried bladderwrack, broken glass,

Pale blue squills and yellow rock roses.
The next low ridge that we climb discloses

One more field for the sheep to graze
While, scarcely seen on this hottest of days,

Far to the eastward, over there,
Snowdon rises in pearl-grey air.

Multiple lark-song, whispering bents,
The thymy, turfy and salty scents

And filling in, brimming in, sparkling and free
The sweet susurration of incoming sea.

*John Betjeman*


## Todd the Backyard King
*(A poem to read aloud – remember to
miaow sweetly at the end.)*

I'm not your fluffy lap-cat
Who purrs to hear you sing;
Your curl-up-on-the-mat-cat
With dainty bell to ring;
Your pretty-pounce-and-pat-cat
Who chases after string . . .
I'm Todd, the catch-a-rat-cat,
The Mighty Backyard King.

I'm not your snooze-and-yawn-cat
With soft and velvet paw;
Your doze-upon-the-lawn-cat
With sheathed and secret paw;
Your slink-about-and-fawn-cat
With meek and milky jaw . . .
I'm Todd, the blood-at-dawn-cat,
Who takes his breakfast RAW.

I'm not your prize-rosette-cat
(My whiskers fray and bend);
I'm not your matching-set-cat
(One ear has lost its end);
I'm not your preen-and-pet-cat
(My coat's too torn to mend) . . .
But when I'm cold-and-wet-cat,
I'm Todd – your fireside friend.

*Clare Bevan*

## Sky's Daughter

If you walk into mist a story begins
If you eat snow snowmen appear in your dreams
If you see the moon in a pond you're nearly grown up
Falling in streams brings you good luck
These are the laws of water, sky's daughter

If you watch a river too long you start to feel old
One cup of water is worth two buckets of gold
If you watch clouds long enough a dragon appears
Icicles don't grow on my grandfather's beard
   These are the laws of water, sky's daughter

If you watch the wild sea you start to grow wise
If you leave a tap running a cactus plant cries
At the centre of whirlpools devils make plans
Goblins hide in watering-cans
   These are the laws of water, sky's daughter

If you stand in puddles it will help you grow tall
If you watch the tides turn you sometimes feel small
Sleeping lakes dream of fish falling through air
Waterfalls are rivers washing their hair
   These are the laws of water, sky's daughter

*Matt Black*

## Facing the Truth – with Haikus

Mr Mackie said,
'Today, you lucky people,
We're doing haikus!'

'What's one of them, sir?'
'Poems to stir the senses,
Plus, they're very short.

23

A mere three lines long
Just seventeen syllables
Simple, pimple – right?

Three lines made up of
Words which are five syllables
Then seven, then five.'

'Haikus,' Alex groaned.
'What a waste of time and space.'
I didn't think so.

'Japanese poems.
Haikus . . .' sighed Mr Mackie.
'A pure, paced rhythm.'

'But sir,' said Alex,
'Haikus mean lots of counting.
That's not fair! That's maths!'

'Haikus are art, child.
Full of heart, soul and passion
So let your mind soar.'

'To where? And what for?'
'To the stars and beyond, child.'
'And when I land, sir?'

Mr Mackie frowned,
Scratched his head and frowned some more.
'You'll have memories.'

'Big deal!' Alex scoffed.
And that was the end of that.
Haikus bit the dust.

*Malorie Blackman*

# Joy

He who binds to himself a joy
Does the wingèd life destroy;
But he who kisses the joy as it flies
Lives in eternity's sun rise.

*William Blake*

# All Lies!

Amy's Dad is twenty feet tall!
Lee's pen is solid gold!
Laura's Mum is the Queen of Egypt!

Lance lives in a tent in the park!
Isabelle's brother has got three eyes!
Elizabeth eats worms for breakfast!
Simon has got a homework doing machine!

*Ian Bland*

## Neighbours

Let me introduce you
To the people on our street,
They're quite the nicest bunch of folks
You'll ever want to meet.

Dan Singh lives at number one,
He's a ballet teacher,
Next door is A. Manning,
The Pentecostal preacher.

That's Mitch Egan at number three,
He's from the USA,
Number four's the tailor and his wife,
Mr and Mrs Hemmingway.

The one outside of number five
Is chatty Miss D. Bate,
She's lived there twenty years now
With her shaky aunt Vi Brayte.

There's the local bobby, D. Fence,
Who married Miss Dee Skreete,
Homes and secrets are all safe,
With these two on our street.

We used to have another cop here,
One called D.C. Eve,
But he wasn't to be trusted,
So we said he had to leave.

That's shy little Miss D. Muir,
In front of number eight,
Next door is Mr B. Hind,
Bless him, he's always late.

Mr Isher at twelve is a cleaner,
And his first name is Paul.
Me? I live at number nine,
And I'm your friend, Noah Hall.

*Valerie Bloom*

## School Sports Day Confession

There was one
Good thing about
Being the Long Jump
Measurer,

You could cheat.

Cheat, not for yourself
But for someone else.
The noblesse Robin Hood
Style cheat.

I gave Margaret Beart
The extra six inches
She needed to win
The 1966 Long Jump

Because I loved her.

*Gary Boswell*


## The Night Has a Thousand Eyes

The night has a thousand eyes,
    And the day but one;
Yet the light of the bright world dies
    With the dying sun.

The mind has a thousand eyes,
    And the heart but one;
Yet the light of a whole life dies
    When love is gone.

*Francis William Bourdillon*

## Ten Slightly Unfamiliar Sayings

There's no smoke without . . . well, a lot
   of bits of wispy stuff floating around in
   the air and smelling as if something's been burned.
Every cloud has . . . an aeroplane in it.

Early to bed and early to rise . . . means
   you miss all the late films on TV.
All work and no play . . . makes Jack a
   completely unbelievable schoolboy.

A stitch in time saves . . . you from
   having to finish that cross-country race.
A friend in need . . . is probably someone
   you should avoid like the plague.
Too many cooks . . . means that you must
   have wandered into a training centre
   for TV chefs, or something.

Money is the root of all evil . . .
   but that's OK so long as I've got plenty.
The family that plays together . . .
   usually ends up having a huge row.
He who laughs last, laughs
   longest . . . unless you stuff an
   old sock in his mouth first.

*Tony Bradman*

## When did I get worse?

'Things aren't what they used to be.'
So say
My Gran and Grandad,
Mum and Dad.
Everything was
Bigger, better, brighter,
Cleaner, calmer, cosier,
Surer, smoother, steadier,
Fairer, fuller, friendlier.
Makes you think –
What about me?

*Redvers Brandling*

## It's Not My Cup of Tea

It's not my cup of tea,
It's just not the thing for me.
Not my burger, not my chips,
Not my spicy salsa dips,
Not my sweet and sour chicken,
It just isn't finger-lickin'.
Not my cheeseburger and fries,
Not my steak and kidney pies,

Not my sausages and fritter,
Not my pizza margarita,
Not my cola, not my juice,
Not my sticky chocolate mousse,
Not my rum-and-raisin ice,
It just isn't very nice.
Really not the thing for me.
No! It's not my cup of tea!

*Paul Bright*


## Fall, Leaves, Fall

Fall, leaves, fall; die, flowers, away;
Lengthen night and shorten day;
Every leaf speaks bliss to me
Fluttering from the autumn tree.

I shall smile when wreaths of snow
Blossom where the rose should grow;
I shall sing when night's decay
Ushers in a drearier day.

*Emily Brontë*

31

## The Soldier

If I should die, think only this of me:
   That there's some corner of a foreign field
That is for ever England. There shall be
   In that rich earth a richer dust concealed;
A dust whom England bore, shaped, made aware,
   Gave, once, her flowers to love, her ways to roam,
A body of England's, breathing English air,
   Washed by the rivers, blest by suns of home.

And think, this heart, all evil shed away,
   A pulse in the eternal mind, no less
      Gives somewhere back the thoughts by England
         given;
Her sights and sounds; dreams happy as her day;
   And laughter, learnt of friends; and gentleness,
      In hearts at peace, under an English heaven.

*Rupert Brooke*

## *Pippa's Song*

The year's at the spring
And day's at the morn;
Morning's at seven;
The hill-side's dew-pearled;
The lark's on the wing;
The snail's on the thorn:
God's in his heaven –
All's right with the world!

*Robert Browning*

## *Saturday Morning Where I Live*

### 1

My brothers are two happy little boys,
And five years old – and twins. That's twice the noise.
My sister plays CDs, and she annoys
My Mum with the loud music she enjoys.

The dog licks out his bowl and barks for more.
My Dad stuffs washing in and slams the door,
And sets our old machine to shake and roar;
It spills his cornflakes on the kitchen floor.

The tv's on, of course, and someone's trying
To sell us things we'd never dream of buying,
And that starts up the neighbours' baby crying
– *And now our shirts and pants are tumble-drying* –!

## 2

But then, quite unexpectedly,
The world begins to change,
And I sense something different,
Special and new and strange.

The twins have settled down to read,
My sister's at the shops,
My Dad switches the telly off,
The baby's crying stops,

The dog's asleep, and for some while
The washing hasn't stirred
– And something enters into my head
I've hardly ever heard:

The sound of silence – like a sea
Without the sound of waves,
– Like mountain tops without the wind,
– Like subterranean caves

Without the echoes – like a sleep
Nothing on earth can break,
Of soldiers in their graves – except
*I'm* living and awake!

Alan Brownjohn

## Jungle Jive

In the jungle chimpanzees
gibber jabber chomping fleas,
and bright lizards look like gemstones
on ginormous jagged leaves,
and plants with hearts like jam tarts
are digesting bugs and bees,
and army ants on journeys
juggle feasts on feet with ease,
and monkeys are enjoying jumps
on a giant gym trapeze,
and birds like jewelled jesters
do the jungle jive in trees.

*Liz Brownlee*

## Upon the Snail

She goes but softly, but she goeth sure;
She stumbles not as stronger creatures do:
Her journey's shorter, so she may endure
Better than they which do much further go.

She makes no noise, but stilly seizeth on
The flower or herb appointed for her food,
The which she quietly doth feed upon,
While others range and gare, but find no good.

And though she doth but very softly go,
However 'tis not fast, nor slow, but sure;
And certainly they that do travel so,
The prize they do aim at, they do procure.

*John Bunyan*

## My Heart's in the Highlands

My heart's in the Highlands, my heart is not here;
My heart's in the Highlands a-chasing the deer;
Chasing the wild deer, and following the roe,
My heart's in the Highlands wherever I go.
Farewell to the Highlands, farewell to the North,
The birth-place of valour, the country of worth;
Wherever I wander, wherever I rove,
The hills of the Highlands for ever I love.

Farewell to the mountains, high covered with snow;
Farewell to the straths and green valleys below;
Farewell to the forests and wild-hanging woods;
Farewell to the torrents and loud-pouring floods.
My heart's in the Highlands, my heart is not here;
My heart's in the Highlands a-chasing the deer;
Chasing the wild deer, and following the roe,
My heart's in the Highlands, wherever I go.

*Robert Burns*

# *So, We'll Go No More A-Roving*

So, we'll go no more a-roving
　　So late into the night,
Though the heart be still as loving
　　And the moon be still as bright.

For the sword outwears its sheath,
　　And the soul wears out the breast,
And the heart must pause to breathe,
　　And love itself have rest.

Though the night was made for loving,
　　And the day returns too soon,
Yet we'll go no more a-roving
　　By the light of the moon.

*Lord Byron*

*C is for . . .*

## *This is not an apple (after Magritte)*

t
h
e
s e
are   words
in   praise   of   those
who   long   ago   planted   the
orchard   and   the   generations
who   trimmed   and   tidied,   swept
and   weeded,   who   helped   the   white
storm   of   blossom   turn   each   year
to   swollen   drops   of   sweetened
rain   which   store   for   winter
the   green   tang   of   spring,
red   flush   of   summer   in
flesh   crisp   and   cool
as   an   autumn   mist
but   this   is   not
an   apple

*Dave Calder*

# Close to the Smiles of a Million Children

Close to the lifeboat which waits in its station
Close to the souvenir stalls by the score
Close to the teashops so crowded with tourists
Close to the kiddies who always want more.

Close to the boxes of fish on the quayside
Close to the trawlers which sail into port
Close to the smiles of a million children
Close to the ice-creams that daddies have bought.

Close to the sound of the seagulls squawking
Close to the bathers enjoying a dip
Close to the cliff paths on which I go walking
Close to the pensioners out on a trip.

Close to the jetty where people sit fishing
Close to the waves which crash on the shore
I sit looking out of my harbour-side cottage
Glad to be close to the seaside once more.

*Richard Caley*

## The Mad Gardener's Song

He thought he saw an Elephant
    That practised on a fife:
He looked again, and found it was
    A letter from his wife.
'At length I realize,' he said,
    'The bitterness of Life!'

He thought he saw a Buffalo
    Upon the chimney-piece:
He looked again, and found it was
    His Sister's Husband's Niece.
'Unless you leave this house,' he said,
    'I'll send for the Police!'

He thought he saw a Rattlesnake
    That questioned him in Greek:
He looked again, and found it was
    The Middle of Next Week.
'The only thing I regret,' he said,
    'Is that it cannot speak!'

He thought he saw a Banker's Clerk
    Descending from the bus:
He looked again, and found it was
    A Hippopotamus:
'If this should stay to dine,' he said,
    'There won't be much for us!'

He thought he saw a Kangaroo
    That worked a coffee-mill:
He looked again, and found it was
    A Vegetable-Pill.
'Were I to swallow this,' he said,
    'I should be very ill!'

He thought he saw a Coach-and-Four
    That stood beside his bed:
He looked again, and found it was
    A Bear without a Head.
'Poor thing,' he said, 'poor silly thing!
    It's waiting to be fed!'

He thought he saw an Albatross
    That fluttered round the lamp:
He looked again, and found it was
    A Penny-Postage-Stamp.
'You'd best be getting home,' he said:
    'The nights are very damp!'

He thought he saw a Garden-Door
    That opened with a key:
He looked again, and found it was
    A Double Rule of Three:
'And all its mystery,' he said,
    'Is clear as day to me!'

He thought he saw an Argument
That proved he was the Pope:
He looked again, and found it was
A Bar of Mottled Soap.
'A fact so dread,' he faintly said,
'Extinguishes all hope!'

*Lewis Carroll*

# Road

*'. . . happiness isn't on the road to anything . . .*
*happiness is the road.'*
**(Bob Dylan, quoting his maternal grandmother)**

Put your ear
against this road
and you will hear
the wheels that rolled

The souls that passed
the stories told
of journeys made
from young to old

The towns that rose
the dreams that fell
the weary resting
by the well

The hopeful going
back for more
the soldier coming
home from war

The horses' hooves
the driving rain
the travellers' tales
the circus train

The songs the cries
the laughs the lies
the lovers lost in
long goodbyes

And though this road
will let you roam
it's always there
to bring you home

*James Carter*

## Freddie Phipps

Freddie Phipps
Liked fish and chips.
Jesse Pinch liked crime.

Woodrow Waters
Liked dollars and quarters.
Paul Small liked a dime.

Sammy Fink
Liked a lemon drink.
Jeremy Jones liked lime.

Mortimer Mills
Liked running down hills.
Jack Jay liked to climb.

Hamilton Hope
Liked water and soap.
Georgie Green liked grime;

But Willy Earls
Liked pretty girls
And had a much better time.

*Charles Causley*

## Let Sleeping Dogs Lie

Hot dogs are toothless, yet prone to bite
And sharp enough to cut the mustard.
They never bark, but if you whisper
'Sausages' – a hissing sound is heard!
Bedded on onions, they satisfy;
Wrapped in rolls, let sleeping hot dogs lie.

*Debjani Chatterjee*

## The Donkey

When fishes flew and forests walked
  And figs grew upon thorn,
Some moment when the moon was blood
  Then surely I was born;

With monstrous head and sickening cry
  And ears like errant wings,
The devil's walking parody
  Of all four-footed things.

The tattered outlaw of the earth,
  Of ancient crooked will:
Starve, scourge, deride me: I am dumb,
  I keep my secret still.

Fools! For I also had my hour;
   One far fierce hour and sweet:
There was a shout about my ears,
   And palms before my feet.

          *G. K. Chesterton*

## *Sheep in Winter*

The sheep get up and make their many tracks
And bear a load of snow upon their backs,
And gnaw the frozen turnip to the ground
With sharp quick bite, and then go noising round
The boy that pecks the turnips all the day
And knocks his hands to keep the cold away
And laps his legs in straw to keep them warm
And hides behind the hedges from the storm.
The sheep, as tame as dogs, go where he goes
And try to shake their fleeces from the snows,
Then leave their frozen meal and wander round
The stubble stack that stands beside the ground,
And lie all night and face the drizzling storm
And shun the hovel where they might be warm.

          *John Clare*

## *i married a monster from outer space*

the milky way she walks around
both feet firmly off the ground
two worlds collide two worlds collide
here comes the future bride
give me a lift to the lunar base
i want to marry a monster from outer space

i fell in love with an alien being
whose skin was jelly whose teeth were green
big bug eyes death-ray glare
feet like flippers and cubic hair
i was over the moon
i asked her back to my place
then i married the monster from outer space

the days were numbered the nights were spent
in a rent-free furnished oxygen tent
a cyborg chef serves up cuisine
the colour of which i've never seen
i needed nutrition to keep up the pace
when i married the monster from outer space

when we walked out tentacle in hand
you could sense that the earthlings would not understand
it was nudge nudge when we got on the bus
they said it's extraterrestrial not like us
it's bad enough with another race
but blimey a monster from outer space

in a cybernetic fit of rage
she took off to another age
she lives beyond recorded time
with a new boyfriend a blob of slime
now every time i see a translucent face
i remember the monster from outer space

*John Cooper Clarke*

# The Strawberry-yogurt Smell of Words

Once we made a telephone
– string, stretched between two yogurt pots.
'Hello? Hello?'
Communication!
You spoke. I heard.

It's a solitary game now,
the thumb-dance of text, beep of fax,
but I still recall the buzz of string,
the strawberry-yogurt
smell of words.

*Mandy Coe*

## *Secret Diary Of The Girl We All Want To Sit Next To When Her Best Friend Is Absent*

Lesson 1 – Music – A new sound greets my ears.
I sat next to Michael.
He was nothing but a twerp
Who thought that I would be impressed to hear him burp.

Lesson 2 – Science – Experiments with the Laws of Gravity
I sat next to Darren,
A freckled faced fool
Who tried for my attention by falling off his stool.

Lesson 3 – Maths – Things just don't add up.
I sat next to Barry
Who gave me a funny look
As he chewed several pages of my exercise book.

Lesson 4 – History – A chance to study a living fossil.
I sat with Samuel
Who was completely unaware
That he missed his mouth at dinnertime and had pasta in
   his hair.

Lesson 5 – English – Penmanship takes on a new meaning.
I sat with Kevin
A chimp in schoolboy clothes
Absolutely irresistible with my biro up his nose.

At home – A moment of quiet reflection.
I sat with no one.
Who will end my sorrow?
I hope my friend's recovered or it's those boys again
   tomorrow

*John Coldwell*

## I saw a stable

I saw a stable, low and very bare,
   A little child in the manger.
The oxen knew Him, had Him in their care,
   To men He was a stranger.
The safety of the world was lying there,
   And the world's danger.

*Mary Coleridge*

## *Kubla Khan*

In Xanadu did Kubla Khan
A stately pleasure-dome decree:
Where Alph, the sacred river, ran
Through caverns measureless to man
   Down to a sunless sea.
So twice five miles of fertile ground
With walls and towers were girdled round:
And there were gardens bright with sinuous rills,
Where blossomed many an incense-bearing tree;
And here were forests ancient as the hills
Enfolding sunny spots of greenery.

But oh! that deep romantic chasm which slanted
Down the green hill athwart a cedarn cover!
A savage place! as holy and enchanted
As e'er beneath a waning moon was haunted
By woman wailing for her demon-lover!
And from this chasm, with ceaseless turmoil seething,
As if this earth in fast thick pants were breathing,
A mighty fountain momently was forced:
Amid whose swift half-intermitted burst
Huge fragments vaulted like rebounding hail,
Or chaffy grain beneath the thresher's flail;
And 'mid these dancing rocks at once and ever
It flung up momently the sacred river.
Five miles meandering with a mazy motion
Through wood and dale the sacred river ran,
Then reached the caverns measureless to man,

And sank in tumult to a lifeless ocean:
And 'mid this tumult Kubla heard from far
Ancestral voices prophesying war!

    The shadow of the dome of pleasure
    Floated midway on the waves;
    Where was heard the mingled measure
    From the fountain and the caves.
It was a miracle of rare device,
A sunny pleasure-dome with caves of ice!
    A damsel with a dulcimer
    In a vision once I saw:
    It was an Abyssinian maid,
    And on her dulcimer she played,
    Singing of Mount Abora.
    Could I revive within me
    Her symphony and song,
    To such a deep delight 'twould win me,
That with music loud and long,
I would build that dome in air,
That sunny dome! those caves of ice!
And all who heard should see them there,
And all should cry, Beware! Beware!
His flashing eyes, his floating hair!
Weave a circle round him thrice,
And close your eyes with holy dread,
For he on honey-dew hath fed,
And drunk the milk of Paradise.

*Samuel Taylor Coleridge*

# Night Owl

Clouds look like broomsticks
with witches riding high,
trees grow grey fingers
to paint away the sky.

Shadows shade night creatures
hiding by each door,
the wind whispers slowly
like a dragon's empty roar.

A star mixes moon dust
dropping dreams below,
tooth fairies fall to earth
guided by their glow.

Children wait for wishes
as a fox starts to howl,
all watched over by the stare
of a wise and distant owl.

*Andrew Collett*

## On Turning Ten

The whole idea of it makes me feel
like I'm coming down with something,
something worse than any stomach ache
or the headaches I get from reading in bad light –
a kind of measles of the spirit,
a mumps of the psyche,
a disfiguring chicken pox of the soul.

You tell me it is too early to be looking back,
but that is because you have forgotten
the perfect simplicity of being one
and the beautiful complexity introduced by two.
But I can lie on my bed and remember every digit.
At four I was an Arabian wizard.
I could make myself invisible
by drinking a glass of milk a certain way.
At seven I was a soldier, at nine a prince.

But now I am mostly at the window
watching the late afternoon light.
Back then it never fell so solemnly
against the side of my tree house,
and my bicycle never leaned against the garage
as it does today,
all the dark blue speed drained out of it.

This is the beginning of sadness, I say to myself,
as I walk through the universe in my sneakers.
It is time to say good-bye to my imaginary friends,
time to turn the first big number.
It seems only yesterday I used to believe
there was nothing under my skin but light.
If you cut me I would shine.
But now when I fall upon the sidewalks of life,
I skin my knees. I bleed.

*Billy Collins*

## Invisible Magicians

Thanks be to all magicians,
The ones we never see,
Who toil away both night and day
Weaving spells for you and me.

The ones who paint the rainbows
The ones who salt the seas
The ones who purify the dew
And freshen up the breeze

The ones who brighten lightning
The ones who whiten snow
The ones who shine the sunshine
And give the moon its glow

The ones who buff the fluffy clouds
And powder blue the skies
The ones who splash the colours on
The sunset and sunrise

The ones who light volcanoes
The ones who soak the showers
The ones who wave the waves
And open up the flowers

The ones who spring the Spring
And warm the Summer air
The ones who carpet Autumn
And frost the Winter earth

The ones who polish icicles
The ones who scatter stars
The ones who cast their magic spells
Upon this world of ours

Thanks to one and thanks to all
Invisible and true
Nature's magic heaven sent
To earth for me and you.

*Paul Cookson*

## *Kindness to Animals*

This poem was commissioned by the editor of *The Orange Dove of Fiji*, an anthology for the benefit of the World Wide Fund for Nature. It was rejected as unsuitable.

If I went vegetarian
And didn't eat lambs for dinner,
I think I'd be a better person
And also thinner.

But the lamb is not endangered
And at least I can truthfully say
I have never, ever eaten a barn owl,
So perhaps I am OK.

*Wendy Cope*

## A Chance in France

'Stay at home,'
Mum said.

But I –
took a chance
in France,
turned grey
for the day
in St Tropez,
I forgot
what I did
in Madrid,
had some tussles
in Brussels
with a trio
from Rio,
lost my way
in Bombay,
nothing wrong
in Hong Kong,
felt calmer
in Palma,
and quite nice
in Nice,
yes, felt finer
in China,
took a room
in Khartoum

and a villa
in Manila,
had a 'do'
in Peru
with a llama
from Lima,
took a walk
in New York
with a man
from Milan,
lost a sneaker
in Costa Rica,
got lumbago
in Tobago,
felt a menace
in Venice,
was a bore
in Singapore,
lost an ear
in Korea,
some weight
in Kuwait,
tried my best
as a guest
in old Bucharest,
got the fleas
in Belize
and came home.

*Pie Corbett*

## The Woodman's Dog

Shaggy, and lean, and shrewd, with pointed ears,
And tail cropped short, half lurcher and half cur –
His dog attends him. Close behind his heel
Now creeps he slow; and now, with many a frisk
Wide-scampering, snatches up the drifted snow
With ivory teeth, or ploughs it with his snout;
Then shakes his powdered coat, and barks for joy.

*William Cowper*

## Peter Grimes

With greedy eye he looked on all he saw;
He knew not justice, and he laughed at law;
On all he marked he stretched his ready hand;
He fished by water, and he filched on land.
Oft in the night has Peter dropped his oar,
Fled from his boat and sought for prey on shore;
Oft up the hedge-row glided, on his back
Bearing the orchard's produce in a sack,
Or farm-yard load, tugged fiercely from the stack;
And as these wrongs to greater numbers rose,
The more he looked on all men as his foes.
　　He built a mud-walled hovel, where he kept
His various wealth, and there he oft-times slept . . .

*from* Peter Grimes, *George Crabbe*

## November Night

Listen . . .
With faint dry sound,
Like steps of passing ghosts,
The leaves, frost-crisped, break from the trees
And fall.

*Adelaide Crapsey*

## The Whistler

My little brother is almost six,
He's good at maths and magic tricks,
He's quite a neat writer,
He can hop and jump and pull funny faces,
He can do top buttons and tie his laces,
He's a fearless fighter.

But he wanted to whistle – and though he tried
Till his face went red and he almost cried,
He still couldn't do it,
So he asked me how and I said: 'Make an O
With your mouth and then, very gently, blow
A whistle through it.'

And he did – but now the trouble is
My little brother practises
All day long,
He sucks in his cheeks, he puffs and blows,
Whatever he's doing, his whistling goes
On and on . . . and on . . .

*June Crebbin*

## *maggie and milly and molly and may*

maggie and milly and molly and may
went down to the beach (to play one day)

and maggie discovered a shell that sang
so sweetly she couldn't remember her troubles, and

milly befriended a stranded star
whose rays five languid fingers were;

and molly was chased by a horrible thing
which raced sideways while blowing bubbles: and

may came home with a smooth round stone
as small as a world and as large as alone.

For whatever we lose (like a you or a me)
it's always ourselves we find in the sea

*e. e. cummings*

## *Pickety Witch*

Pickety Witch, Pick-Pickety Witch
Picka, Picka, Pickety Witch.

Which wicked witch went every which way?
Which stayed behind? Don't know. Can't say.

Which boiling cauldron bubbled magic spells?
Which ones just simmered and made nasty smells?

Which witch's wand shot stars far and wide?
Which ones hung limp as a worm that's just died?

Which witch's cat could whistle and bark?
Which ones were scared to go out in the dark?

Which witch's broomstick streamed to the sky?
Which ones went backwards? Don't ask me why!

Which witch has lifted the Superwitch Cup
While the rest of the coven gave in and gave up?

Pickety Witch, it's Pickety Witch
Picka, Picka, Pickety Witch.

*Jennifer Curry*

# D is for . . .

## 'I've Eaten Many Strange and Scrumptious Dishes . . .'

'I've eaten many strange and scrumptious dishes in my
    time,
Like jellied gnats and dandyprats and earwigs cooked in
    slime,
And mice with rice – they're really nice
When roasted in their prime.
(But don't forget to sprinkle them with just a pinch of
    grime.)

'I've eaten fresh mudburgers by the greatest cooks there
    are,
And scrambled dregs and stinkbugs' eggs and hornets
    stewed in tar,
And pails of snails and lizards' tails,
And beetles by the jar.
(A beetle is improved by just a splash of vinegar.)

'I often eat boiled slobbages. They're grand when served
    beside
Minced doodlebugs and curried slugs. And have you ever
    tried
Mosquitoes' toes and wampfish roes
Most delicately fried?
(The only trouble is they disagree with my inside.)

'I'm mad for crispy wasp-stings on a piece of buttered toast,
And pickled spines of porcupines. And then a gorgeous
   roast
Of dragon's flesh, well hung, not fresh –
It costs a pound at most,
(And comes to you in barrels if you order it by post.)

'I crave the tasty tentacles of octopi for tea
I like hot-dogs, I LOVE hot-frogs, and surely you'll agree
A plate of soil with engine oil's
A super recipe.
(I hardly need to mention that it's practically free.)

'For dinner on my birthday shall I tell you what I chose:
Hot noodles made from poodles on a slice of garden
   hose –
And a rather smelly jelly
Made of armadillo's toes.
(The jelly is delicious, but you have to hold your nose.)

'Now comes,' *the Centipede declared*, 'the burden of my
   speech:
These foods are rare beyond compare – some are right out
   of reach;
But there's no doubt I'd go without
A million plates of each
For one small mite,
One tiny bite
Of this FANTASTIC PEACH!'

*Roald Dahl*

## *D is for Dog*

My dog went mad and bit my hand,
  I was bitten to the bone:
My wife went walking out with him,
  And then came back alone.

I smoked my pipe, I nursed my wound,
  I saw them both depart:
And when my wife came back alone,
  I was bitten to the heart.

W. H. Davies

## *Nativity*

When God decided to be bones and skin and blood like
  us
He didn't choose a palace, nothing grand – no frills and
  fuss.
He slipped in through the back door, with the straw and
  hay and dust.
He just became a baby with no choice but to trust,
And love us without question, as every baby must.

But Creation knew the wonder of this tiny newborn king.
The crystal depths of space were touched, the air itself
    would sing.
The Word is flesh. The silence of the glittering stars is
    shattered. Heaven rings.
The sky blazed wild with angels, whose song was fire and
    snow
When God lay in his mother's arms two thousand years
    ago.

*Jan Dean*

## The Scarecrow

All winter through I bow my head
    Beneath the driving rain;
The North Wind powders me with snow
    And blows me black again;
At midnight in a maze of stars
    I flame with glittering rime,
And stand, above the stubble, stiff
    As mail at morning-prime.
But when that child, called Spring, and all
    His host of children, come,
Scattering their buds and dew upon
    These acres of my home,
Some rapture in my rags awakes;
    I lift void eyes and scan

The skies for crows, those ravening foes,
   Of my strange master, Man.
I watch him striding lank behind
   His clashing team, and know
Soon will the wheat swish body high
   Where once lay sterile snow;
Soon shall I gaze across a sea
   Of sun-begotten grain,
Which my unflinching watch hath sealed
   For harvest once again.

*Walter de la Mare*

## Bending . . . The Truth!

Did you see how well I hit that ball,
   The way I made it swerve,
How quick it zipped around the wall,
   That little bit of curve,
The pace, the dip, the curl, the whip,
   How skilfully I bent it?
Now that's what I'd call craftsmanship . . .
   If only I had *meant it!*

*Graham Denton*

## *We All Have To Go*

The sound drew nearer;
a wheezy, hoarse breathing
as if some heavy weight
were being dragged along.
There was a smell of burnt bones.
A horny, hairy finger edged
round the trickling, slimy wall.
Then a large warty nose,
topped by bloodshot watery eyes,
slowly emerged from the gloom.
The eyes widened, glowing
to a bright red.
Its pace quickened and soon
it towered above us.
The huge slavering mouth opened –
'Any of you lot know where
the toilet is?'

*John C. Desmond*

## A Word is Dead

A word is dead
When it is said,
Some say.
I say it just
Begins to live
That day.

*Emily Dickinson*


## Missing Important Things

I didn't go to school this week
I stayed at home with Dad.
I didn't do a work sheet
and I am really rather glad.
I didn't do the number work,
I didn't do my words,
I didn't learn my spellings
and I didn't read my page.
I didn't go to school today –
we fixed the shed instead,
tied some flies and feathers
and dug the onion bed.
I saw the cat have kittens,
I climbed right up a tree,

mixed some sand and water
and held a bumble bee.
I didn't go to school all week
and I'm really not too sad –
I missed important lessons
and stayed at home with Dad.

*Peter Dixon*

## The Duck

I hope you may have better luck
Than to be bitten by the Duck.

This bird is generally tame,
But he is dangerous all the same;

And though he looks so small and weak,
He has a very powerful beak.

Between the hours of twelve and two
You never know what he may do.

And sometimes he plays awkward tricks
From half-past four to half-past six.

And any hour of the day
It's best to keep out of his way.

*Lord Alfred Douglas*

## Beware The Bush

prise wide your eyes, plug up your nose,

They try to snag you by the clothes,

through which her threatening fingers poke.

at dusk she dresses in a cloak

she plays a trick, a crafty game:

Beware the bush, the very same,

whispering, lisping shy, soft sounds.

a gentle maid in leafy gown

At night this bush does not remain

Beware the bush in Lurkin Lane!

twang at your tonsils, tweak your ears

snatch out your teeth and smear your tears . . .

You'll feel her floppy tongue upon

your cheeks! Your neck! You'll want to run

but wrists and ankles are entwined –

the more you pull the more you'll find

her tendril twigs are tightening

round chest and shoulders, under chin.

You're choking! Coughing! Turning blue!

Amazing what a bush can do.

*Gina Douthwaite*

## Happy the Man

Happy the man, and happy he alone,
   He who can call today his own;
He who, secure within, can say,
   Tomorrow, do thy worst, for I have lived today.

*John Dryden*

## The Famous

What do the famous have for breakfast?
I think they have pale pink eggs
laid by rare birds, lightly boiled,
served by uniformed maids.

Then I think they have a bath, the famous,
in tubs with diamond taps.
They soak in perfumed lemonade
and their maids scrub their backs.

Then what? The famous get dressed, of course,
in gold and silver clothes
and go out for the day. They sail around
on the Thames in glass-bottomed boats,

waving at children on bridges,
while menservants fish for sturgeon
and scoop out the caviar with silver spoons
to feed to the famous for luncheon.

At bedtime the famous have stories
written specially by famous writers,
then they sleep and dream of being famous
in their sparkling pyjamas or nighties.

*Carol Ann Duffy*


## Sound Advice

'Come inside at once,' Mum said.
'Get out of all that rain.'
'We're having fun,' was our reply,
'don't be such a pain.'

'It's raining cats and dogs,' Mum cried.
I told her, 'Don't be silly.'
Just then a sopping Labrador
squashed flat my brother Willie.

*Michael Dugan*

## *playground haiku*

Everyone says our
playground is overcrowded
but I feel lonely

*Helen Dunmore*

## *Hiding Places*

While she counts to a hundred
through a veil of fingers

you are breathing red velvet
behind the stairway curtain
soaking up living-room murmurs of aunts
pretending they don't know where you are.

Or you are crouching behind Dad's shed
among water-butt toads and stinky compost,
mossy window frames and waving branches
outstaring next door's ever curious cat.

Or you are squeezing between heavy-scented lilac
and your playhouse window
trying not to give the game away
with your reflection in the glass.

Or you are flattening against the house wall,
beyond where a chimney breast juts out,
fingers reddening with brick dust,
risking the sudden hellos of nosy neighbours.

Or you are scrunching inside the airing cupboard
arms tight round the water tank
stifling giggles and whispers
among warm fluff and watery gurgles.

Or you are curling under the spare bed
in space the Hoover never reaches
among lost toys and magazines,
dolls' legs and silent dust.

You must not move
even though your nose is tickling,
your foot is itching,
your breath is trembling.

Any minute now
she could come creeping
near
nearer
and find you.

*Sue Dymoke*

# *E is for . . .*

## The Lion and Albert

There's a famous seaside place called Blackpool,
    That's noted for fresh air and fun,
And Mr and Mrs Ramsbottom
    Went there with young Albert, their son.

A grand little lad was young Albert,
    All dressed in his best; quite a swell
With a stick with an 'orse's 'ead 'andle,
    The finest that Woolworth's could sell.

They didn't think much to the Ocean:
    The waves, they was fiddlin' and small,
There was no wrecks and nobody drownded,
    Fact, nothing to laugh at at all.

So, seeking for further amusement,
    They paid and went into the Zoo,
Where they'd Lions and Tigers and Camels,
    And old ale and sandwiches too.

There were one great big Lion called Wallace;
    His nose were all covered with scars –
He lay in a somnolent posture,
    With the side of his face on the bars.

Now Albert had heard about Lions,
　　How they was ferocious and wild –
To see Wallace lying so peaceful,
　　Well, it didn't seem right to the child.

So straightway the brave little feller,
　　Not showing a morsel of fear,
Took his stick with its 'orse's 'ead 'andle
　　And pushed it in Wallace's ear.

You could see that the Lion didn't like it,
　　For giving a kind of a roll,
He pulled Albert inside the cage with 'im,
　　And swallowed the little lad 'ole.

Then Pa, who had seen the occurrence,
　　And didn't know what to do next,
Said, 'Mother! Yon Lion's et Albert,'
　　And Mother said, 'Well, I am vexed!'

Then Mr and Mrs Ramsbottom –
　　Quite rightly, when all's said and done –
Complained to the Animal Keeper,
　　That the Lion had eaten their son.

The keeper was quite nice about it;
　　He said, 'What a nasty mishap.
Are you sure that it's *your* boy he's eaten?'
　　Pa said, 'Am I sure? There's his cap!'

The manager had to be sent for.
    He came and he said, 'What's to do?'
Pa said, 'Yon Lion's et Albert,
    And 'im in his Sunday clothes, too.'

Then Mother said, 'Right's right, young feller;
    I think it's a shame and a sin,
For a lion to go and eat Albert,
    And after we've paid to come in.'

The manager wanted no trouble,
    He took out his purse right away,
Saying, 'How much to settle the matter?'
    And Pa said, 'What do you usually pay?'

But Mother had turned a bit awkward
    When she thought where her Albert had gone.
She said, 'No! Someone's got to be summonsed' –
    So that was decided upon.

Then off they went to the P'lice Station,
    In front of the Magistrate chap;
They told 'im what happened to Albert,
    And proved it by showing his cap.

The Magistrate gave his opinion
    That no one was really to blame
And he said that he hoped the Ramsbottoms
    Would have further sons to their name.

At that Mother got proper blazing,
  'And thank you, sir, kindly,' said she.
'What, waste all our lives raising children
  To feed ruddy Lions? Not me!'

*Marriott Edgar*

## Some Favourite Words

Mugwump, chubby, dunk and whoa,
Swizzle, doom and snoop,
Flummox, lilt and afterglow,
Gruff, bamboozle, whoop
And nincompoop.

Wallow, jungle, lumber, sigh,
Ooze and zodiac,
Innuendo, lullaby,
Ramp and mope and quack
And paddywhack.

Moony, undone, lush and bole,
Inkling, tusk, guffaw,
Waspish, croon and cubby-hole,
Fern, fawn, dumbledore
And many more . . .

*Richard Edwards*

## Macavity: The Mystery Cat

Macavity's a Mystery Cat: he's called the Hidden Paw –
For he's the master criminal who can defy the Law.
He's the bafflement of Scotland Yard, the Flying Squad's
    despair:
For when they reach the scene of crime – *Macavity's not*
    *there!*

Macavity, Macavity, there's no one like Macavity,
He's broken every human law, he breaks the law of gravity.
His powers of levitation would make a fakir stare,
And when you reach the scene of crime – *Macavity's not*
    *there!*
You may seek him in the basement, you may look up in
    the air –
But I tell you once and once again, *Macavity's not there!*

Macavity's a ginger cat, he's very tall and thin;
You would know him if you saw him, for his eyes are
    sunken in.
His brow is deeply lined with thought, his head is highly
    domed;
His coat is dusty from neglect, his whiskers are uncombed.
He sways his head from side to side, with movements like
    a snake;
And when you think he's half asleep, he's always wide
    awake.

Macavity, Macavity, there's no one like Macavity,
For he's a fiend in feline shape, a monster of depravity.
You may meet him in a by-street, you may see him in the
    square –
But when a crime's discovered, then *Macavity's not there!*

He's outwardly respectable. (They say he cheats at cards.)
And his footprints are not found in any file of Scotland
    Yard's.
And when the larder's looted, or the jewel-case is rifled,
Of when the milk is missing, or another peke's been stifled,
Or the greenhouse glass is broken, and the trellis past
    repair –
Ay, there's the wonder of the thing! *Macavity's not there!*
And when the Foreign Office find a Treaty's gone astray,
Or the Admiralty lose some plans and drawings by the
    way,
There may be a scrap of paper in the hall or on the stair –
But it's useless to investigate – *Macavity's not there!*
And when the loss has been disclosed, the Secret Service
    say:
'It *must* have been Macavity!' – but he's a mile away.
You'll be sure to find him resting, or a-licking of his
    thumbs,
Or engaged in doing complicated long division sums.

Macavity, Macavity, there's no one like Macavity,
There never was a Cat of such deceitfulness and suavity.
He always has an alibi, and one or two to spare:
At whatever time the deed took place – MACAVITY
   WASN'T THERE!
And they say that all the Cats whose wicked deeds are
   widely known
(I might mention Mungojerrie, I might mention
   Griddlebone)
Are nothing more than agents for the Cat who all the time
Just controls their operations: the Napoleon of Crime!

*T. S. Eliot*

## Black cat

Sleepy-purred cat peers out
from the nest of my duvet
eyes glinting green gold black.

He yawns
mouth prawnpink.

Settles.

Sleek black paw
over coal black nose
and sleeps.

*Suzanne Elvidge*

## Letters

Every day brings a ship,
Every ship brings a word;
Well for those who have no fear,
Looking seaward, well assured
That the word the vessel brings
Is the word they wish to hear.

*Ralph Waldo Emerson*

*F is for . . .*

## What the Donkey Saw

No room in the inn, of course,
And not that much in the stable,
What with the shepherds, Magi, Mary,
Joseph, the heavenly host –
Not to mention the baby
Using our manger as a cot.
You couldn't have squeezed another cherub in
For love or money.

Still, in spite of the overcrowding,
I did my best to make them feel wanted.
I could see that the baby and I
Would be going places together.

*U. A. Fanthorpe*

## Books

What worlds of wonder are our books!
As one opens them and looks,
New ideas and people rise
In our fancies and our eyes.

The room we sit in melts away,
And we find ourselves at play
With someone who, before the end,
May become our chosen friend.

Or we sail along the page
To some other land or age.
*Here's* our body in the chair,
But our mind is over *there*.

Each book is a magic box
Which with a touch a child unlocks.
In between their outside covers
Books hold all things for their lovers.

*Eleanor Farjeon*

# Look Out!

The witches mumble horrid chants,
You're scolded by five thousand aunts,
  A Martian pulls a fearsome face
  And hurls you into Outer Space,
You're tied in front of whistling trains,
A tomahawk has sliced your brains,
  The tigers snarl, the giants roar,
  You're sat on by a dinosaur.
In vain you're shouting 'Help' and 'Stop',
The walls are spinning like a top,
  The earth is melting in the sun
  And all the horror's just begun.
And, oh, the screams, the thumping hearts
That awful night before school starts.

*Max Fatchen*

## Haiku Through the Year

Secret snow at night:
Morning's a muffled white world.
Let's go out in it!

These are waiting days.
Branch and twig lie sealed and black:
They're dreaming of leaves.

Blackthorn, daffodils,
Primroses and celandines:
Yes, Spring's on the March.

April. Just the word
Has the freshness of the month.
Repeat it: April.

Apple blossom month:
A hesitant pink and white.
Summer May start here.

Self-pick strawberries.
We've already stuffed ourselves:
Can't face them for tea.

Let's get up early
And breathe the coolness before
The day's cloudless blaze.

No school in August!
Thirty-one days of heaven.
We're off to the sea!

Summer still holds but
Now September doubts creep in.
The evening's chilly.

Golden October.
Let's just go down to the woods
And look at beech trees.

The evening's hazy.
Is it a November mist,
Or smoke from bonfires?

December nightfall:
Fine snow on a bitter wind.
Houses huddle down.

*Eric Finney*

## I dream of a time

I dream of a time

When the only blades are blades of corn
When the only barrels are barrels of wine
When the only tanks are full of water
When the only chains are chains of hands

I hope for a time. . . .

*John Foster*

## A Fishy Thought

A kipper
With a zipper
Would be neater
For the eater . . .

*Vivian French*

## A Prayer in Spring

Oh, give us pleasure in the flowers today;
And give us not to think so far away
As the uncertain harvest; keep us here
All simply in the springing of the year.

Oh, give us pleasure in the orchard white,
Like nothing else by day, like ghosts by night;
And make us happy in the happy bees,
The swarm dilating round the perfect trees.

And make us happy in the darting bird
That suddenly above the bees is heard,
The meteor that thrusts in with needle bill,
And off a blossom in mid-air stands still.

For this is love and nothing else is love,
The which it is reserved for God above
To sanctify to what far ends He will,
But which it only needs that we fulfil.

*Robert Frost*

## Advice to Children

Caterpillars living on lettuce
Are the colour of their host:
Look out, when you're eating a salad,
For the greens that move the most.

Close your mouth tight when you're running
As when washing you shut your eyes,
Then as soap is kept from smarting
So will tonsils be from flies.

If in spite of such precautions
Anything nasty gets within,
Remember it will be thinking:
'Far worse for me than him.'

*Roy Fuller*

# G *is for* . . .

## The Ancient Wizard's Daughter

Over hill and dale and water
Flies the Ancient Wizard's daughter.

On her broomstick sits her cat;
On her head, her witch's hat.

She knows all her father's magic
But won't use it, which is tragic

(So her father thinks), but she
Doesn't care, for she can see

All the world spread out below
As she flies. She swoops down low,

Sees the tiniest creatures run
Among the grasses, in the sun.

Flies up high towards the stars,
Visits Venus, Saturn, Mars.

Everywhere she calls her home.
She has all the earth to roam.

All the beauty of the world
Beneath her broomstick is unfurled.

Over hill and dale and water
Flies the Ancient Wizard's daughter,

Sees the magic in all things:
Needs no spells: her heart has wings.

*Pam Gidney*


## Elegy on the Death of a Mad Dog

Good people all, of every sort,
 Give ear unto my song;
And if you find it wondrous short,
 It cannot hold you long.

In Islington there was a man,
 Of whom the world might say,
That still a godly race he ran,
 Whene'er he went to pray.

A kind and gentle heart he had,
 To comfort friends and foes;
The naked every day he clad,
 When he put on his clothes.

And in that town a dog was found,
 As many dogs there be,
Both mongrel, puppy, whelp, and hound,
 And curs of low degree.

This dog and man at first were friends;
   But when a pique began,
The dog, to gain some private ends,
   Went mad and bit the man.

Around from all the neighbouring streets
   The wondering neighbours ran,
And swore the dog had lost his wits,
   To bite so good a man.

The wound it seemed both sore and sad
   To every Christian eye;
And while they swore the dog was mad,
   They swore the man would die.

But soon a wonder came to light,
   That showed the rogues they lied:
The man recovered of the bite –
   The dog it was that died.

*Oliver Goldsmith*

## *Boots*

It's chilly on the touch line, but
with all my kit on
underneath my clothes
I'm not too cold. Besides,
I've got a job to do:
   I'm Third Reserve
   I run the line.

I've been the Third Reserve all season,
every Saturday.
I've never missed a match.
At Home, Away:
It's all the same to me:
   'Cos I'm the third Reserve,
   The bloke who runs the line.

That's my reward
for turning up
to every practice session, every
circuit training. Everything.
No one else does that –
   To be the Third Reserve,
   To run the line.

No chance of substitutions.
Broken ankles on the pitch
mean someone else's chance, not mine.
One down –
                    and still two more to go:
    When you're the Third Reserve
    You run the line.

When I was first made Third Reserve
my dad and me went out
and bought new boots. I keep them in the box.
I grease them every week and put them back.
    When you're the Third Reserve –
    you know the score –
You run the line in worn-out daps.

*Mick Gowar*

## *Presence of Mind*
### *Poem to read when considering an adventure holiday*

When, with my little daughter Blanche,
I climbed the Alps, last summer,
I saw a dreadful avalanche
About to overcome her;
And, as it swept her down the slope,
I vaguely wondered whether
I should be wise to cut the rope
That held us twain together.

I must confess I'm glad I did,
But still I miss the child – poor kid!

*Harry Graham*

## *The* Alice Jean

One moonlit night a ship drove in,
    A ghost ship from the west,
Drifting with bare mast and lone tiller;
    Like a mermaid drest
In long green weed and barnacles
    She beached and came to rest.

All the watchers of the coast
    Flocked to view the sight;
Men and women, streaming down
    Through the summer night,
Found her standing tall and ragged
    Beached in the moonlight.

Then one old woman stared aghast;
    'The *Alice Jean?* But no!
The ship that took my Ned from me
    Sixty years ago –
Drifted back from the utmost west
    With the ocean's flow?

'Caught and caged in the weedy pool
  Beyond the western brink,
Where crewless vessels lie and rot
  In waters black as ink,
Torn out at last by a sudden gale –
  Is it the *Jean*, you think?'

A hundred women gaped at her,
  The menfolk nudged and laughed,
But none could find a likelier story
  For the strange craft
With fear and death and desolation
  Rigged fore and aft.

The blind ship came forgotten home
  To all but one of these,
Of whom none dared to climb aboard her:
  And by and by the breeze
Veered hard about, and the *Alice Jean*
  Foundered in foaming seas.

*Robert Graves*

# H *is for . . .*

## The World is a Box

My heart is a box of affection.
My head is a box of ideas.
My room is a box of protection.
My past is a box full of years.

The future's a box full of after.
An egg is a box full of yolk.
My life is a box full of laughter
And the world is a box full of folk.

*Sophie Hannah*

## Some Things the Grown-ups Just Won't Tell You

Why doesn't a ball stay up there
When you throw it up in the air?
That tortoise that we've got at school
Why doesn't it grow hair?
I wish I knew the answers,
I don't think that it's fair.
There's some things that the grown-ups just won't tell you.

Why don't little ball-bearings
Grow up to be big?
Why can't you get bits of bacon
And make them back into pig?
They say they don't know the answers,
But I think that that's a fib.
There's some things that the grown-ups just won't tell you.

Where does all the fluff come from
You find between your toes?
How do those big bogeys
Climb inside your nose?
They must come in the night
When you're asleep, I suppose.
There's some things that the grown-ups just won't tell you.

Does God go to the toilet?
And what gives you a cough?
Why don't fish get rusty?
What puts the smell in your socks?
If you undid your belly-button,
Would your bum really fall off?
There's some things that the grown-ups just won't tell you.

Why doesn't rain fall sideways?
Or even upside down?
Where do the stars go in the daytime?
Why do worms live underground?

You eat food all different colours,
Why does it all come out brown?
There's some things that the grown-ups just won't tell you.

*Mike Harding*

## The Fallow Deer at the Lonely House

One without looks in to-night
    Through the curtain-chink
From the sheet of glistening white;
One without looks in to-night
    As we sit and think
    By the fender-brink.

We do not discern those eyes
    Watching in the snow;
Lit by lamps of rosy dyes
We do not discern those eyes
    Wondering, aglow,
    Fourfooted, tiptoe.

*Thomas Hardy*

## A Story of Snowballs

Only last week down by the canal
I met Shiner Smith, my very best pal
A cold winter's day filled up with snow
The water was grey, the going was slow.

We both felt so bored, there was nothing to do
But then a small pleasure craft chugged into view
A big man with a beard was steering the boat
Wrapped up in a scarf and a thick overcoat.

Shiner looked hard at this nautical bloke
Said 'Let's chuck a snowball, just for a joke'.
'You what?' I replied, 'You wouldn't dare'
But one had already whizzed through the air!

So I scraped up some snow hard in my fist
The boat hardly moved, it couldn't be missed
I gave my packed snowball one final squeeze
Then shouted 'Oy Fatty, have one of these!'

He was so angry, red-faced and sore
He felt even worse when we threw twenty more
He shouted 'Hey stop that. Just pack it in!'
And Shiner got him, smack on the chin.

I landed a beauty right down his neck
Another one burst like a bomb on his deck
He slipped on the bits, lost his footing and fell
Bounced like a ball and gave a loud yell.

We lobbed him some others, ran from the path
Into the woods and had a good laugh
Then we said goodbye and soon forgot
About our sad sailor and the soaking he got.

Several days later school started again
I was feeling OK, so was Shiner, but when
We walked through the gate and over the yard
We noticed our teacher glaring quite hard.

Beside him there stood a man that we knew
Last time we'd seen him he'd turned the air blue
Shouting and yelling through a big beard
I started to feel shaky and weird.

He snarled 'Glad to meet you. Just couldn't wait
I'm your new headteacher, I'm Mr Tate
So you like to play snowballs?' he said with a sneer
'Well I'd like to have a word in your ear.'

'I hope you enjoyed your moment of fun
I've just phoned your parents to say what you've done
But this time my friends it's my turn to win.
In fact here they are! Come in! Let's begin!

*David Harmer*

## *Haircut*

What I hate
about having a haircut
is being asked
how I want it
when I don't want it cut at all.

What I hate
about having a haircut
is being asked
questions with
the whole room listening to my answers.

What I hate
about having a haircut
is being asked
to look in
the mirror and say how I like it.

What I hate most
about having a haircut
is going to school
and everyone
telling me I've had my hair cut.

*Michael Harrison*

# The Railway Children

When we climbed the slopes of the cutting
We were eye-level with the white cups
Of the telegraph poles and the sizzling wires.

Like lovely freehand they curved for miles
East and miles west beyond us, sagging
Under their burden of swallows.

We were small and thought we knew nothing
Worth knowing. We thought words travelled the wires
In the shiny pouches of raindrops.

Each one seeded full with the light
Of the sky, the gleam of the lines, and ourselves
So infinitesimally scaled

We could stream through the eye of a needle.

*Seamus Heaney*

## Uncle and Auntie

My auntie gives me a colouring book and crayons
I begin to colour
after a while auntie leans over and says
you've gone over the lines
what do you think they're for
eh?
some kind of statement is it?
going to be a rebel are we?
your auntie gives you a lovely present
and you have to go and ruin it
I begin to cry
my uncle gives me a hanky and some blank paper
do some doggies of your own he says
I begin to colour
when I have done
he looks over
and says they are all very good
he is lying
only some of them are

*John Hegley*

## *Through another day*

I slouch and mumble through another day

realize I've forgotten my Maths homework
which I didn't actually do

dream up new excuses
for forgetting my Maths homework
without letting on that I haven't done it

get told off for texting in class

repeat 'I'm so bored'
as a motto and reason for everything

whilst meanwhile
in the astral amphitheatre

high above
this small square of earth

enormous giants
face each other

supergigantic stars called
Alpha and Beta
so big that we need
a new word for big

Alpha and Beta
red and blue opponents
with the energy output
of thousands upon thousands upon thousands of suns
like neverending Maths
which I can't add up
and which I couldn't do anyway

and all fantastically meaningful

although I don't know what it means

they're above us
now
in the burning there

whilst I'm in this little here
offering a pathetic story
as to why I've forgotten my Maths homework
which I didn't do anyway.

*Stewart Henderson*

## The Cullen Skink

*I came upon Cullen Skink in a Scottish cookery book. It's really a dish of smoked haddock, but I imagined it was the name of a strange creature. I like the poem's mystery. I like the idea of someone 'skinking' and the poem says quite a lot about how I often feel inside.*

If the temperature's right
you might see him out
in a very fine suit
of the best bravado,
but skinking with caution
for his eyesight's poor
and he's all out of proportion.

Unshelled, in the buff,
his raw-pink skin
is prone to shrinkage
which is why he lets no one in
and lives far north, alone
in a nest of coddled mementoes
kept on simmer. Some say
it's the Cullen Skink's nature
to shiver and to be perpetually
on the brink of some great thought
he never delivers.

He likes to drink.
He likes to look at the moon.
At night you can hear the clink
as he walks the jetty
trailing a kind of umbilical cord,
the dried-up remnants
of wings, fur, paws.

*Diana Hendry*

## The Dark

I don't like the dark coming down on my head
It feels like a blanket thrown over the bed
I don't like the dark coming down on my head

I don't like the dark coming down over me
It feels like the room's full of things I can't see
I don't like the dark coming down over me

There isn't enough light from under the door
It only just reaches the edge of the floor
There isn't enough light from under the door

I wish that my dad hadn't put out the light
It feels like there's something that's just out of sight
I wish that my dad hadn't put out the light

But under the bedclothes it's warm and secure
You can't see the ceiling you can't see the floor
Yes, under the bedclothes it's warm and secure
So I think I'll stay here till it's daylight once more.

*Adrian Henri*

## Dreams

Here we are all, by day; by night we are hurled
By dreams, each one into a several world.

*Robert Herrick*

## Sally

She was a dog-rose kind of girl:
elusive, scattery as petals;
scratchy sometimes, tripping you like briars.
She teased the boys
turning this way and that, not to be tamed
or taught any more than the wind.
Even in school the word 'ought'
had no meaning for Sally.
On dull days
she'd sit quiet as a mole at her desk

127

delving in thought.
But when the sun called
she was gone, running the blue day down
till the warm hedgerows prickled the dusk
and moths flickered out.

Her mother scolded; Dad
gave her the hazel-switch,
said her head was stuffed with feathers
and a starling tongue.
But they couldn't take the shine out of her.
Even when it rained
you felt the sun saved under her skin.
She'd a way of escape
laughing at you from the bright end of a tunnel,
leaving you in the dark.

*Phoebe Hesketh*

## Homework

Homework sits on top of Sunday, squashing Sunday flat.
Homework has the smell of Monday, homework's very fat.
Heavy books and piles of paper, answers I don't know.
Sunday evening's almost finished, now I'm going to go
Do my homework in the kitchen. Maybe just a snack,
Then I'll sit right down and start as soon as I run back
For some chocolate sandwich cookies. Then I'll really do

All that homework in a minute. First I'll see what new
Show they've got on television in the living room.
Everybody's laughing there, but misery and gloom
And a full refrigerator are where I am at.
I'll just have another sandwich. Homework's very fat.

*Russell Hoban*

## Brother

I had a little brother
And I brought him to my mother
And I said I want another
Little brother for a change.
But she said don't be a bother
so I took him to my father
And I said this little bother
Of a brother's very strange.

But he said one little brother
Is exactly like another
And every little brother
Misbehaves a bit he said.
So I took the little brother
From my mother and my father
And I put the little bother
Of a brother back to bed.

*Mary Ann Hoberman*

## *No!*

No sun – no moon!
No morn – no noon –
No dawn – no dusk – no proper time of day –
No sky – no earthly view –
No distance looking blue –
No road – no street – no 't'other side the way' –
No end to any Row –
No indications where the Crescents go –
No top to any steeple –
No recognitions of familiar people –
No courtesies for showing 'em –
No knowing 'em! –
No travelling at all – no locomotion,
No inkling of the way – no notion –
'No go' – by land or ocean –
No mail – no post –
No news from any foreign coast –
No Park – no Ring – no afternoon gentility –
No company – no nobility –
No warmth, no cheerfulness, no healthful ease,
No comfortable feel in any member –
No shade, no shine, no butterflies, no bees,
No fruits, no flowers, no leaves, no birds –
November!

*Thomas Hood*

## Pied Beauty

Glory be to God for dappled things –
 For skies of couple-colour as a brinded cow;
  For rose-moles in all stipple upon trout that swim;
Fresh-firecoal chestnut-falls; finches' wings;
 Landscape plotted and pieced – fold, fallow, and plough;
  And áll trádes, their gear and tackle and trim.
All things counter, original, spare, strange;
 Whatever is fickle, freckled (who knows how?)
  With swift, slow; sweet, sour; adazzle, dim;
He fathers-forth whose beauty is past change:
          Praise him.

*Gerard Manley Hopkins*


## The Elephant or, The Force of Habit

A tail behind, a trunk in front,
Complete the usual elephant.
The tail in front, the trunk behind
Is what you very seldom find.

If you for specimens should hunt
With trunks behind and tails in front,
That hunt would occupy you long;
The force of habit is so strong.

*A. E. Housman*

131

## The Trees Dance

Forest-father, mighty Oak:
*On my back the lightning-stroke*

Spear-maker, Ash-tree:
*Safely cross the raging sea*

Black-eyed Elder, crooked-arm:
*Break me and you'll come to harm*

Dark Yew, poison-cup:
*Keep the ghosts from rising up*

Summer's herald, Hawthorn, May:
*Home of the fairies, keep away*

Cry-a-leaf, the bitter Willow:
*Where you walk at night I follow*

Slender Hazel, water-hound:
*In my nutshell wisdom found*

Birch the dancer, best broom:
*Sweep the evil from your room*

Fair Apple, fire's sweet wood:
*Dreams of power and poets' food*

Winter-shiner, Holly the king:
*Good cheer to the cold I bring*

Rowan the guard, berry-red:
*Fairies fear and witches dread*

*Libby Houston*

## Final Curve

When you turn the corner
And you run into *yourself*
Then you know that you have turned
All the corners that are left.

*Langston Hughes*

## The Harvest Moon

The flame-red moon, the harvest moon,
Rolls along the hills, gently bouncing,
A vast balloon,
Till it takes off, and sinks upward
To lie in the bottom of the sky, like a gold doubloon.

133

The harvest moon has come,
Booming softly through heaven, like a bassoon.
And earth replies all night, like a deep drum.

So people can't sleep,
So they go out where elms and oak trees keep
A kneeling vigil, in a religious hush.
The harvest moon has come!

And all the moonlit cows and all the sheep
Stare up at her petrified, while she swells
Filling heaven, as if red hot, and sailing
Closer and closer like the end of the world

Till the gold fields of stiff wheat
Cry 'We are ripe, reap us!' and the rivers
Sweat from the melting hills.

*Ted Hughes*


## Houses

I remember the houses –

David Bullen's
where I used to say to his mother
'I'm hungry'
and get a sugar butty;

134

Norman Watkinson's next door
with the grandfather clock
watching from the stairs,
sawdust on the kitchen floor
and an old pump in the garden
groaning and coughing up
glittering water.

I'd two grandads' houses to go in,

one with a goose in the garden,
a harmonium with two pedals in the front room,
and an aeroplane propeller
propped up behind the big four-poster bed;

the other had freshly painted carts
to look at and not touch in the paint-shop,
with shafts held up high
and glistening blue and gold lettering,
next to coffins standing waiting.

The houses I visit now
are warmer and posher and neater
and less interesting.

*Robert Hull*

*I is for . . .*

## *Limerick*

A limerick's cleverly versed –
The second line rhymes with the first;
The third one is short,
The fourth's the same sort,
And the last line is often the worst.

*John Irwin*

*J is for . . .*

## The Dream of the Plastic Bag

The plastic bag in the gutter
Looked up at the moon
And said, 'Yes,
I'd rather be a balloon.

Perhaps if I could be
Rounder, puffier, stronger,
Tighter, airier,
Just a lovelier vision of me.'

A breath, a gust of air
Bounced it along the pavement,
Lifted it, bobbing and tumbling
Lightly along the wall top

And away into the night sky.

*Lucinda Jacob*

## *Fighting the Tide*

On holidays, after seven and a half months
of counting the days since Christmas
(Easter is good – but there's only
so much fun in chocolate eggs),
after the excited sing-song journey
and me being sick, 'Every twenty miles!'
according to my dad,
we would go to the beach every day of the fortnight
and eat sandy sandwiches,
packets of family-size crisps – each,
swig Coke,
stuff 99s,
and each a whole chicken, or ham,
or at the end of the fortnight, a tin of spam,
between us.
The rest ate whole tomatoes,
(but not me, I don't like them –
'Fussy eater', my nan says).
But my favourite part of every day was
fighting the tide.
My sister, my brother and I would build
huge walls of sand,
defences against the battery of the tide's attack.
The design would change every time with
each of us arguing whether a pointed end would
stay standing longer than a rounded wall.
There was no time to decorate these sea walls
with castellations or crenellations,
towers or gates.

The onslaught of the tide was there to be fought.
We lost.
Every day.
But every day
we fought
just the same.

In the evening we would sit in the bar with the adults
fighting the tide of sleep.

At the end of the fortnight, I would fight the tide of leaving.

Part of me is always with my brother and sister, fighting
   the tide.

*Huw James*

## The Black Cat's Conversation

Do not suppose,
Because I keep to the fire,
Am out half the night,
Sleep where I fall,
Eye you with stares
Like your finest marbles,
That I am not conscious
Of your slightest changes
In mood. I never
Miss your temper
Although you attempt

To disguise it. I know

How envious you are
Of my lithe body,
My lack of self-consciousness,
My glossy coat,
My imperious air.
All this is instinct,
Something you've lost
Except when you cower
From the rats I bring in,
Proud of my haul.
I am proud of my pride
And I always win.

*Elizabeth Jennings*

## Solo Flight

Looks like a long, long, long way down
to the ground.
Sounds
like a long, long, long way down
to the ground.

Something says
I'm sure to be safe,
because I'm a baby bat,

but,
but,
but I think I'll hang around
for an itsy-bitsy bat-bit longer.

No!
Why, mum, why?
Time flies
and so must I . . .

Well, if you say so,
first time solo,
here I go.                                        I can fly!

    Here I go.                                    I can fly!

        Here I go.                                I can fly.

                o                    o

                    o            o

                o        o

                    o

                                        *Mike Johnson*

147

## About Friends

The good thing about friends
is not having to finish sentences.

I sat a whole summer afternoon with my friend once
on a river bank, bashing heels on the baked mud
and watching the small chunks slide into the water
and listening to them – plop plop plop.
He said, 'I like the twigs when they . . . you know . . .
like that.' I said, 'There's that branch . . . '
We both said, 'Mmmm.' The river flowed and flowed
and there were lots of butterflies, that afternoon.

I first thought there was a sad thing about friends
when we met twenty years later.
We both talked hundreds of sentences,
taking care to finish all we said,
and explain it all very carefully,
as if we'd been discovered in places
we should not be, and were somehow ashamed.

I understood then what the river meant by flowing.

*Brian Jones*

# from *Witches' Song*

The owl is abroad, the bat and the toad,
   And so is the cat-a-mountain;
The ant and the mole sit both in a hole,
   And frog peeps out o' the fountain;
The dogs they do bay, and the timbrels play,
   The spindle is now a-turning;
The moon it is red, and the stars are fled,
   And all the sky is a-burning.

*Ben Jonson*

## Towards the End of Summer

Cherry red and honey bee
Buzzed around the summer flowers
Bumbled round the luscious fruits.
Patient weaver clambered by.

Silently while the others bobbed
And busied in the bright blue air
Hither, zither, merrily,
Weaver waved his cool brown arms
And gently drew around the tree
Silken skeins so fine so fine

No one could see that they were there,
Until one Autumn morning when
Cherry was gone and bee asleep
A silver shawl was laced across the grass
With little beads like pearls strung all along.

*Jenny Joseph*

# K *is for . . .*

## An Old Woman's Fire

I remember watching my grandmother build her fire
The honest kindling, the twisted newspaper,
The tiny tower of good black coal.
And how, once lit, she'd hold a sheet of newspaper
Across the fire and say, 'Watch it suck, dear.'

I remember the way my grandmother loved to poke her
    fire
Always nudging the coals and turning them over
opening the grate, placing another jet jewel on the glowing
    fire
and how she'd fuss over the dying embers.

I remember how she sat there in her armchair,
Her old face, a little pink and flushed from the heat.
And how she'd smile at her coal fire, lovingly,
And sigh, 'There's nothing like a real fire is there dear?'

As if her life could have been something else entirely.

*Jackie Kay*

## There Was a Naughty Boy

There was a naughty boy,
A naughty boy was he,
He would not stop at home,
He could not quiet be –
He took
In his knapsack
A book
Full of vowels
And a shirt
With some towels,
A slight cap
For night cap,
A hair brush,
Comb ditto,
New stockings –
For old ones
Would split O!
This knapsack
Tight at 's back
He riveted close
And followed his nose
To the North,
To the North,
And followed his nose
To the North.

There was a naughty boy,
  And a naughty boy was he,
He ran away to Scotland
  The people for to see –
    There he found
    That the ground
    Was as hard,
    That a yard
    Was as long,
    That a song
    Was as merry,
    That a cherry
    Was as red –
    That lead
    Was as weighty,
    That fourscore
    Was as eighty,
    That a door
    Was as wooden
    As in England –
So he stood in his shoes
  And he wondered,
    He wondered,
He stood in his shoes
  And he wondered.

  *John Keats*

## The ways of words

Words can streak snappily,
purposeful as swallows
in summer,

soaring

flipping twisting

dipping

twittering to brood filled

nests

under eaves,
filling us with the excitement
of their energy.

Words can plod half-heartedly
dull as the life of the donkey
circling the well,
or drearily dim as wintry water
without a single swan.

Words can be
old friends
we love to be with
remembering

the old stories
the old fears
the old laughs
as fresh as yesterday.

**ANGRY** words
attack us inwardly,
startling us into intense response,
while soft words
whisper soothing thoughts,
as gentle as giraffes.

Words sometimes make us
c
r
y

salt tears of joy or sorrow.

And just once in a while
words
and sparks fierce fireworks
in bursts of stars flaring brief
explode in
brilliance

a dazzle of electrifying images.

*Penny Kent*

## *Apple Crumble*

I like Apple Crumble –
it sticks on to the spoon.
I'd eat it every morning
and every afternoon,
I'd eat it for my breakfast,
for supper, lunch or tea . . .
Yes, I like apple crumble;
just pass me some, and see!

Apple Crumble's
    fine and tasty,
Apple Crumble's
    nice.
you can serve it
hot and steamy,
or as cold
    as ice.
You can swallow it
    in pieces
and in dollops
    too;
you can gulp it,
chew it, bite it
like the tigers
    do.
You can have it
    smooth and creamy,

crisp and brown
   on top –
GO ON MAKING
   Apple Crumble!
Never, never
   stop,
for I couldn't
   and I wouldn't
say 'No thank you' . . .

   WHAT?

You're not baking
   ANY PUDDING?

Did you say
   you're NOT?

   *Jean Kenward*

# The Sands of Dee

O Mary, go and call the cattle home,
   And call the cattle home,
   And call the cattle home
  Across the sands of Dee;'
The western wind was wild and dank with foam,
   And all alone went she.

The western tide crept up along the sand,
    And o'er and o'er the sand,
    And round and round the sand,
  As far as eye could see.
The rolling mist came down and hid the land:
  And never home came she.

'Oh, is it weed, or fish, or floating hair –
    A tress of golden hair,
    A drownèd maiden's hair
  Above the nets at sea?
Was never salmon yet that shone so fair
  Among the stakes on Dee.'

They rowed her in across the rolling foam,
    The cruel, crawling foam,
    The cruel, hungry foam,
  To her grave beside the sea:
But still the boatmen hear her call the cattle home,
  Across the sands of Dee.

*Charles Kingsley*

## *Look Back in Wonder*

Though the Elephant's behind
Is delightfully designed
And the rump of any Rhino's mighty fine,
Though the buttocks of a Bear
Are indubitably fair
And the Pig is fundamentally divine,
Though the bum of any Bison
Is a singularly nice un,
And the backside of a Boa never stops –
Yet not one's got such a bottom as
The hugeous Hippopotamus.
For bottoms, Hippopotami are tops.

*Dick King-Smith*

## The Way Through the Woods

They shut the road through the woods
Seventy years ago.
Weather and rain have undone it again,
And now you would never know
There was once a road through the woods
Before they planted the trees.
It is underneath the coppice and heath
And the thin anemones.
Only the keeper sees
That, where the ring-dove broods,
And the badgers roll at ease,
There was once a road through the woods.

Yet, if you enter the woods
Of a summer evening late,
When the night-air cools on the trout-ringed pools
Where the otter whistles his mate,
(They fear not men in the woods,
Because they see so few.)
You will hear the beat of a horse's feet,
And the swish of a skirt in the dew,
Steadily cantering through
The misty solitudes,
As though they perfectly knew
The old lost road through the woods . . .
But there is no road through the woods.

*Rudyard Kipling*

## A Fistful of Pacifists

A thimbleful of giants
A rugby scrum of nuns
An atom of elephants
A cuddle of guns

A rustle of rhinoceros
A barrel of bears
A swear box of politicians
A bald patch of hairs

A stumble of ballet dancers
A flutter of whales
A mouthful of silence
A whisper of gales

A pocketful of earthquakes
A conference of pears
A fistful of pacifists
A round-up of squares

*David Kitchen*

## Come Camping

Come camping, come camping,
It's really great,
With spider-flavoured sausages
And slugs stuck to your plate.
There are earwigs in your wellingtons
And ants sharing your bed,
The wasps you sprayed are fighting back
And targeting your head.
The hollow where you pitched your tent
Has turned into a bog,
And that dripping muddy monster
Is what used to be your dog.
Your clothes are cold and smelly
Your sleeping bag feels damp,
It's a riot, it's sensational,
So come with us and camp!

*Daphne Kitching*

## Really Really

I find it very hard to read.
So sometimes I pretend,
Just turning pages one by one
Until I reach the end.

Teacher tries to help me;
Knows just what I need.
Sounding words out one by one,
I really want to read.

I really, really want to read
Bright books there on the shelf.
I like it when Miss reads to me,
But I want to read myself.

I know there's magic locked in books,
Princes, places, birds.
That's why I try so very hard
To understand the words.

One day I know I'll really read
A book from start to end.
I won't just turn the pages.
I won't have to pretend.

*John Kitching*

## The Final Kick

Our only ball was lofted
beyond the keeper's fingertips,
high above the crossbar
and clear of the trees to finish
wallop! in the river
                        – before
we had a chance to bully
someone in the water, the current
took its trophy

downstream
towards the sea
where I believe
it's drifting even now
around the oceans of the world,
orbiting the planet like a brand-new moon.

*Stephen Knight*

## Unfolding Bud

One is amazed
By a water-lily bud
Unfolding
With each passing day,
Taking on a richer colour
And new dimensions.

One is not amazed,
At a first glance,
By a poem,
Which is as tight-closed
As a tiny bud.

Yet one is surprised
To see the poem
Gradually unfolding,
Revealing its rich inner self,
As one reads it
Again
And over again.

*Naoshi Koriyama*

# L *is for* . . .

## Taking Care of Business

Today, in a sky as blue as a starling's egg,
The sun is shining brightly
And meringue-white clouds drift away
Like a grazing flock of legless sheep.

A big sycamore ripples green muscles
In the same breeze which harvests blossom
From the late-flowering cherry tree
And scatters frail pinknesses
Over a precise lawn.

Blackbirds and thrushes evict worms
From dark subterranean homes
And squadrons of swept-wing swallows
Blitz clouds of midges along the river
Where a spindle-legged heron waits
Patiently for finger-length trout
To make the wrong move.

A cat stretches in the sunlight
Raking its claws down a wooden post
Then yawns and recurls itself
Into a neat furry package
And closes almond eyes
As Spring gets ready to hand
Summer its inheiritance.

Season trading with season.
Life goes on and on
And although we can't feel it,
Beneath our feet
Our beautiful, ancient
Planet keeps on turning.

Turning.
Taking care
Of business

*Tony Langham*

## Take One Home for the Kiddies

On shallow straw, in shadeless glass,
Huddled by empty bowls, they sleep:
No dark, no dam, no earth, no grass –
Mam, get us one of them to keep.

Living toys are something novel,
But it soon wears off somehow.
Fetch the shoebox, fetch the shovel –
Mam, we're playing funerals now.

*Philip Larkin*

## Family Doctor

My grandpa thinks he's a cricket ball.
And, sometimes, he's a bat.
He went and told the Doctor
And the Doctor said, 'Howzat?'

My sister went to the Doctor's,
In front of the Doctor she sat.
She said, 'Doctor, I think I'm invisible!'
And the Doctor said, 'Who said that?'

My uncle went to the Doctor's
'I'm a toadstool!' I heard him shout.
The Doctor said, 'You're a fun guy.
There's not mushroom for doubt!'

My father went to the Doctor's,
He said, 'I'm feeling chronic!
All I can think of is "Gin, gin, gin!"'
And the Doctor said, 'You need a tonic!'

My brother went to the Doctor's,
He was feeling under the weather.
He said, 'I think I'm some curtains!'
She said, 'Pull yourself together!'

*Ian Larmont*

## The Rainbow

Even the rainbow has a body
made of the drizzling rain
and is an architecture of glistening atoms
built up, built up
yet you can't lay your hand on it,
nay, nor even your mind.

*D. H. Lawrence*

## Reedy River

Ten miles down Reedy River
   A pool of water lies,
And all the year it mirrors
   The changes in the skies.
Within that pool's broad bosom
   Is room for all the stars;
Its bed of sand has drifted
   O'er countless rocky bars.

Around the lower edges
   There waves a bed of reeds,
Where water-rats are hidden
   And where the wild-duck breeds;
And grassy slopes rise gently
   To ridges long and low,
Where the groves of wattle flourish
   And native bluebells grow.

Beneath the granite ridges
   The eye may just discern
Where Rocky Creek emerges
   From deep green banks of fern;
And standing tall between them,
   The drooping she-oaks cool
The hard, blue-tinted waters
   Before they reach the pool.

Ten miles down Reedy River
   One Sunday afternoon,
I rode with Mary Campbell
   To that broad, bright lagoon;
We left our horses grazing
   Till shadows climbed the peak,
And strolled beneath the she-oaks
   On the banks of Rocky Creek.

Then home along the river
 That night we rode a race,
And the moonlight lent a glory
 To Mary Campbell's face;
I pleaded for my future
 All through that moonlight ride,
Until our weary horses
 Drew closer side by side.

Ten miles from Ryan's Crossing
 And five below the peak,
I built a little homestead
 On the banks of Rocky Creek;
I cleared the land and fenced it
 And ploughed the rich red loam;
And my first crop was golden
 When I brought Mary home.

Now still down Reedy River
 The grassy she-oaks sigh;
The waterholes still mirror
 The pictures in the sky;
The golden sand is drifting
 Across the rocky bars;
And over all for ever
 Go sun and moon and stars.

But of the hut I builded
   There are no traces now,
And many rains have levelled
   The furrows of my plough.
The glad bright days have vanished;
   For sombre branches wave
Their wattle-blossom golden
   Above my Mary's grave.

*Henry Lawson*

## Limerick

There was a Young Lady whose eyes,
Were unique as to colour and size;
When she opened them wide,
People all turned aside,
And started away in surprise.

*Edward Lear*

## *The Shining*

That day when I was on the shore,
out further than I'd been before
I found a place all to myself
closed in by rocks and cliff,
where the only sound was lapping water
my steps, the seagull's laughter.

Hard sand and rocks went shelving steep
into clear water, cold and deep . . .
and deeper, darker, pure and still.
The sky was grey, the air was chill –
it seemed the same as it would be
with nobody on earth to see.

This was the kind of hidden nook
where you find treasure – in one look,
millions of pebbles, smooth and round
from age on age of being ground
against each other, to make them shine,
waiting for me to make them mine.

But seemed like something not to touch
in a museum or empty church,
kept from everyone, under glass,
beauties, set inside their case,
glistening with every colour
each one different from each other.

I had to take one – some – to keep –
but the moment each was in my grip
they changed to mere wet weights of stone,
everything I wanted – gone –
faded – damp, pale, grey, and dry.
It was enough to make you cry.

Just one came home with me, that still
sits in the dust on my window sill;
and though they say, just throw it out,
I remember the shining of it,
and wonder, what other things might shine
and still be mine, and still be mine.

*Brian Lee*


# The Question

If I could teach you how to fly
Or bake an elderberry pie
Or turn the sidewalk into stars
Or play new songs on an old guitar
Or if I knew the way to heaven
The names of night, the taste of seven
And owned them all, to keep or lend –
Would you come and be my friend?

You cannot teach me how to fly.
I love the berries but not the pie.
The sidewalks are for walking on,
And an old guitar has just one song.
The names of night cannot be known,
The way to heaven cannot be shown.
You cannot keep, you cannot lend –
But still I want you for my friend.

*Dennis Lee*


## Night Spinner

A spider spinning her web one night
Wove in some silver starlight bright
Then caught some drops
Of moon-washed rain
And threaded them
Into a crystal chain.

Crystal and silver
Crystal and silver
Laced between leaves
On the autumn trees.

Silver and crystal
Silver and crystal
Shivering
Shimmering
In the dawn breeze.

*Patricia Leighton*

## The Dragon Speaks

Now I keep watch on the gold in my rock cave
In a country of stones: old, deplorable dragon,
Watching my hoard. In winter night the gold
Freezes through tough scales my cold belly;
Jagged crowns, cruelly twisted rings,
Icy and knobb'd, are the old dragon's bed.

Often I wish I had not eaten my wife
(Though worm grows not to dragon till he eats worm).
She could have helped me, watch and watch about,
Guarding the gold; the gold would have been safer.
I could uncoil my tired body and take
Sometimes a little sleep when she was watching.

Last night under the moonset a fox barked,
Startled me; then I knew I had been sleeping.
Often an owl flying over the country of stones
Startles me; then I think that I must have slept,
Only a moment. That very moment a Man
Might have come from the towns to steal my gold . . .

They have no pity for the old, lugubrious dragon.
Lord that made the dragon, grant me thy peace,
But say not that I should give up the gold,
Nor move, nor die. Others would have the gold.
Kill rather, Lord, the Men and the other dragons;
Then I can sleep; go when I will to drink.

*C. S. Lewis*

## *And Even Now*

When I was a child,
Lying in bed on a summer evening,
The wind was a tall sweet woman
Standing beside my window.
She came whenever my mind was quiet.

But on other nights
I was tossed about in fear and agony
Because of goblins poking at the blind,
And fearful faces underneath my bed.
We played a horrible game of hide-and-seek
With Sleep the far-off, treacherous goal.

And even now, stumbling about in the dark,
I wonder, Who was it that touched me? –
*What thing laughed?*

*Dorothy Livesay*

## Poem For My Sister

My little sister likes to try my shoes,
to strut in them,
admire her spindle-thin twelve-year-old legs
in this season's styles.
She says they fit her perfectly,
but wobbles
on their high heels, they're
hard to balance.

I like to watch my little sister
playing hopscotch, admire the neat hops-and-skips of her,
their quick peck,
never-missing their mark, not
over-stepping the line.
She is competent at peever.

I try to warn my little sister
about unsuitable shoes,
point out my own distorted feet, the callouses,
odd patches of hard skin.
I should not like to see her
in my shoes.
I wish she would stay
sure footed,
  sensibly shod.

*Liz Lochhead*

## Sunset

The summer sun is sinking low;
  Only the tree-tops redden and glow;
Only the weather-cock on the spire
Of the village church is a flame of fire;
  All is in shadow below.

*Henry Wadsworth Longfellow*

## By the Lake

The great carp cruise the lake
like sharks, breaking the sunlit surface,
lunging for damselflies.

Stealthily, the heron glides
across the water, landing by shallows,
leans like an angle-poise and waits.

People move slowly in the heat
follow the margins, lie in the shade
for hours, choosing their moment –

stalk the dense shrubbery,
winding paths – close swiftly
on the ices, the cream tea.

*Tony Lucas*

# M *is for . . .*

# The Sea
### *An endless song to while away long journeys*

Pools prink plip
Ripples ring rocks
Surf sings softly
Fat foam flecks
White waves whip
Breakers beat boulders
Wind wildly whistles
Waves whack wallop
Wind wildly whistles
Breakers beat boulders
White waves whip
Fat foam flecks
Surf sings softly
Ripples ring rocks
Pools prink plip

*Kevin McCann*

## Wouldn't It Be Funny
## If You Didn't Have a Nose?

You couldn't smell your dinner
If you didn't have a nose
You couldn't tell a dirty nappy
From a summer rose
You couldn't smell the ocean
Or the traffic, I suppose
Oh wouldn't it be funny
If you didn't have a nose?

You couldn't smell your mummy
If you didn't have a nose
You couldn't tell an orange
From a row of smelly toes
You couldn't smell the burning
(Think how quick a fire grows)
Wouldn't it be funny
If you didn't have a nose?

*Where would we be without our hooters?*
*Nothing else would really suit us.*
*What would we sniff through?*
*How would we sneeze?*
*What would we wipe*
*Upon our sleeves?*

You couldn't smell a rat
If you didn't have a nose
You couldn't tell a duchess
From a herd of buffaloes
And . . . mmmm that Gorgonzola
As it starts to decompose
Oh wouldn't it be funny
If you didn't have a nose?

*Where would we be without our hooters?*
*Nothing else would really suit us.*
*And think of those who*
*Rub their noses*
*Life would be tough for*
*Eskimoses*

You couldn't wear your glasses
If you didn't have a nose
And what would bullies aim for
When it came to blows?
Where would nostrils be without them?
When it's runny how it glows
Oh wouldn't it be funny
If you didn't have a . . .
     have a . . .
     have a . . .
         a . . .
         a . . . choo!

*Roger McGough*

## First Appearance of a Superhero in a Book

*(From 'A Child's Lovely Box of Happy Verses', 1598)*

Af the peafantf cowered in their hovelf
and a madman ftole their pigf
a handfome fquire climbed off hif horfe
in bright red hofe and golden wig.

'I am Fuper Fquire Dogoodneff!'
he faid, and then he fang hif fong:
and he fang all fifty verfef
and the fong waf rather long.

And af he fang, the madman
ran off with hif booty
af the peafantf liftened to the fong,
it waf their ferfly duty.

When the fong waf ended
the Fquire faid, 'That'f my fong
now let'f catch the villain!'
But 'twaf too late for he had gone.

Fo Fuper Fquire Dogoodneff
climbed on hif fteed.
'He if ufeleff, Fquire Dogoodneff,'
the peafantf all agreed!

*Ian McMillan*

## Why Old People Say the Things They Do When Young People Ask Them How They Are

Mustn't grumble
Can't complain
Not too bad, thanks
Much the same
Bright as a button
or the sun
Perky
I'm ninety-one years young!
Fit as a fiddle
Sharp as a knife
Never felt better
in all my life.
I'm glad you asked
But I'll keep it snappy
And briefly tell you
That I'm quite happy.
If I had more time
I'd tell you the truth
But I don't want to waste it
Like I did in my youth.

*Lindsay MacRae*

## *When the Funfair Comes to Town*

See the coloured lights that flash,
hear the dodgems when they crash,
give the coconuts a bash
    when the Funfair comes to town,
    when the Funfair comes to town.

Smell the burgers, peas and pies,
wear a mask with wobbly eyes,
throw a hoop and win a prize
    when the Funfair comes to town,
    when the Funfair comes to town.

See the crowds come in and out,
hear the children squeal and shout,
climb aboard the roundabout
    when the Funfair comes to town,
    when the Funfair comes to town.

Taste the toffee you can share,
hear loud music in the air,
ride the Ghost Train . . . if you dare
    when the Funfair comes to town,
    when the Funfair comes to town.

*Wes Magee*

## Cat in the Dark

Mother, Mother, what was that?
Hush, my darling! Only the cat.
(Fighty-bitey, ever-so-mighty)
Out in the moony dark.

Mother, Mother, what was that?
Hush, my darling! Only the cat.
(Prowly-yowly, sleepy-creepy,
Fighty-bitey, ever-so-mighty)
Out in the moony dark.

Mother, Mother, what was that?
Hush, my darling! Only the cat.
(Sneaky-peeky, cosy-dozy,
Prowly-yowly, sleepy-creepy,
Fighty-bitey, ever-so-mighty)
Out in the moony dark.

Mother, Mother, what was that?
Hush, my darling! Only the cat.
(Patchy-scratchy, furry-purry,
Sneaky-peeky, cosy-dozy,
Prowly-yowly, sleepy-creepy,
Fighty-bitey, ever-so-mighty)
Out in the moony dark.

*Margaret Mahy*

# Sea Fever

I must go down to the seas again, to the lonely sea and
the sky,
And all I ask is a tall ship and a star to steer her by,
And the wheel's kick and the wind's song and the white
sail's shaking,
And a grey mist on the sea's face, and a grey dawn
breaking.

I must go down to the seas again, for the call of the
running tide
Is a wild call and a clear call that may not be denied;
And all I ask is a windy day with the white clouds flying,
And the flung spray and the blown spume, and the sea-
gulls crying.

I must go down to the seas again, to the vagrant gypsy life,
To the gull's way and the whale's way where the wind's
like a whetted knife;
And all I ask is a merry yarn from a laughing fellow-rover,
And quiet sleep and a sweet dream when the long trick's
over.

*John Masefield*

### Fragment

My father lifted
a mouthorgan up
to the wind on a hill

and the wind of Bohemia
sighed a few
frail and blue notes

man and child
in a harebell light
frail ghosts . . . faint tune

*Gerda Mayer*

## Giving Thanks Giving Thanks

Giving thanks giving thanks
for rain and rainbows
sun and sunsets
cats and catbirds
larks and larkspur

giving thanks giving thanks
for cows and cowslips
eggs and eggplants
stars and starlings
dogs and dogwood

195

giving thanks giving thanks
for watercress on riverbanks
for necks and elbows knees and shanks
for towers basins pools and tanks
for pumps and handles lifts and cranks

giving thanks giving thanks
for ropes and coils and braids and hanks
for jobs and jokes and plots and pranks
for whistles bells and plinks and clanks
giving giving giving *thanks*

*Eve Merriam*

## Onamatapia

Onamatapia!
Thud-Wallop-**CRASH**!
Onamatapia!
Snip-Snap **GNASH**!
Onamatapia!
Wack-thud-**BASH**!
Onamatapia!
Bong-Ting-**SPLASH**!

*Spike Milligan*

## I like to swing on my own

Crowds are fun on the roundabout
And you need two on the Park see-saw
But when it comes to the swing in my garden:
That's what some quiet is for.

I like to swing in the garden;
I like to watch the ground go by;
I like to see the blackberry bush
And then, all of a sudden, the sky.

I like to go high on my garden swing
When I'm almost upside-down!
Then I sit as it rocks me forth and back . . .
Till my feet can touch the ground again . . .
Till my feet can touch the ground.

*Trevor Millum*


## Ode To My Nose

O Nose
Why perch upon my Face?
Could you not find
A better place?

You jut between
One Eye and tother
So neither Eye
Can see his Brother.

An easy target
For the hostile Fist.
You're an obstruction
When I want to be kissed.

And when you run
It's always South
Over my top lip
Into my Mouth.

O Nose
Why perch upon my Face?
Could you discover
No better place?

My Nose replied:
Up here I have come
As far as possible
From your Bum.

*Adrian Mitchell*

## *Plum*

Don't be so glum,
plum.

Don't feel beaten.

You were made
to be eaten.

But don't you know
that deep within,
beneath your juicy flesh
and flimsy skin,

you bear a mystery,
you hold a key,

you have the making of
a whole new tree.

*Tony Mitton*

## Another Day on the Beach

*If the wind changes*
*you'll be stuck with that face for ever*
*and won't it teach you a lesson.*
They certainly didn't like my
sour-puss, beetle-browed
*I've had enough of this* expression.

Oh to get away from it all,
an outgrown sandcastle king
with his bucket and spade regalia.
If I put my mind to it, though,
and dug deep enough
I could manage a smile in Australia.

                                        *John Mole*

## The Loch Ness Monster's Song

Sssnnnwhuffffll?
Hnwhuffl hhnnwfl hnfl hfl?
Gdroblboblhobngbl gbl gl g g g g glbgl.
Drublhaflablhaflubhafgabhaflhafl fl fl –
gm grawwwww grf grawf awfgm graw gm.
Hovoplodok-doplodovok-plovodokot-doplodokosh?
Splgraw fok fok splgrafhatchgabrlgabrl fok splfok!

Zgra kra gka fok!
Grof grawff gahf?
Gombl mbl bl –
blm plm,
blm plm,
blm plm,
blp.

*Edwin Morgan*

# A to Z

A up said me dad,
B off to bed with you.
C it's half past eight and I've
Decided that from now on it's bed before nine.
E can't be serious I thought.
F he carries on like this I'll never see any TV
G I'll lose my grasp of American slang.
H not fair.
I won't go.
J think I should protest?
K I will.
L o said me dad,
M not standing for this
N y kid thinks he can disobey me has got another think
    coming.
O yes he has!

P, then wash your hands and face, do your teeth and
   straight to bed.
Q then, your sisters will have finished soon.
R you ready yet? Wash that face properly
S pecially round your nose. It's disgusting.
T? No you can't. If you drink tea now you will wet the
   bed
U will you know.
V end of a perfect day. Now I'll tuck you in
W up to save space. Then I can fit your brother in too –
   and the dog and hamster. There you all fit in
Xactly
Y don't you like it? It's cosy, space-saving, economical.
   Go to sleep. Not a peep Do exactly as I
ZZZZZZZZZZZZZZZzz.

*Michaela Morgan*

## Our Ditch

I sat and thought one day
of all the things we'd done
with our ditch; how we'd jumped across
at its tightest point, till I slipped
and fell, came out smelling,
then laid a pole from side to side,
dared each other to slide along it.
We fetched out things that others threw in,

lobbed bricks at tins, played Pooh-sticks.
We buried stuff in the mud and the gunge
then threatened two girls with a ducking.
We floated boats and bombed them,
tiptoed along when the water was ice,
till something began to crack, and we scuttled back.
We borrowed Mum's sieve from the baking drawer,
scooped out tadpoles into a jar
then simply forgot to put them back.
(We buried them next to the cat.)

Then one slow day in summer heat
we followed our ditch to where it began,
till ditch became stream, and stream
fed river, and river sloped off to the sea.
Strange, we thought, our scrap of water
growing up and leaving home,
roaming the world and lapping
at distant lands.

*Brian Moses*

## *In the Attic*

Even though we know now
your clothes will never
be needed, we keep them,
upstairs in a locked trunk.

Sometimes I kneel there,
holding them, trying to relive
time you wore them, to remember
the actual shape of arm and wrist.

My hands push down between
hollow, invisible sleeves,
hesitate, then lift
patterns of memory:

a green holiday, a red christening,
all your unfinished lives
fading through dark summers,
entering my head as dust.

*Andrew Motion*

# N *is for* . . .

## Year 6 Residential

We hiked a hundred miles
(Sir said five)

Got stuck in a bog
(Lucky to be alive)

Made our beds
(Though I can't imagine why)

Cooked our own food
(AAARRRGGGHHH I'm going to die)

Climbed a perilous mountain
(Well, a hill)

Nearly drowned in canoes
(Utterly brill)

Got chased by a (probably cloned)
Killer sheep

The only thing we didn't do
Was sleep.

*Frances Nagle*

## The Hippopotamus

Behold the hippopotamus!
We laugh at how he looks to us,
And yet in moments dank and grim
I wonder how we look to him.
Peace, peace, thou hippopotamus!
We really look all right to us.
As you no doubt delight the eye
Of other hippopotami.

*Ogden Nash*

## The Door
### *(with apologies to Miroslav Holub!)*

Do not open the door!
Maybe inside there is
a seething cauldron,
a wild-tailed dragon,
or a teacher's eye, staring . . .

Do not open the door!
Maybe a snake slithers,
four walls
like an invisible clock
tick away
a never-ending morning.
A teacher's tongue
wags in the darkness
with *your* name on its tip . . .

Do not open the door!
Maybe the ghost of Voldemort
lurks in the shadows,
waiting . . .

Do not open the door!
Maybe
through the breathing darkness
a gnarled, insistent finger
silently unfurls to point
to someone . . .

It
has chosen

*YOU!*

*Judith Nicholls*

## Book-Heart

The books I love
are well fingered and thumbed
have tiny butter smudges
may harbour a crumb
the odd cat-whisker
a few dog-ears
a drop of tear
a brownish stain
(that looks suspiciously like tea)

I for one am glad to say,
do not judge a book
by its cover –
but flit first among its leaves
like a hummingbird
sipping at a flower

The books I love I must admit
do not sit with perfect spines
behind a museum of glass.
No the books I love
get kissed and squeezed
and pressed against my heart.

*Grace Nichols*

## The Moon Is Up

The moon is up: the stars are bright:
  The wind is fresh and free!
We're out to seek for gold tonight
  Across the silver sea!
The world is growing grey and old:
  Break out the sails again!
We're out to seek a Realm of Gold
  Beyond the Spanish Main.

We're sick of all the cringing knees,
  The courtly smiles and lies!
God, let thy singing Channel breeze
  Lighten our hearts and eyes!
Let love no more be bought and sold
  For earthly loss or gain;
We're out to seek an Age of Gold
  Beyond the Spanish Main.

Beyond the light of far Cathay,
  Beyond all mortal dreams,
Beyond the reach of night and day
  Our El Dorado gleams,
Revealing – as the skies unfold –
  A star without a stain,
The Glory of the Gates of Gold
  Beyond the Spanish Main.

*Alfred Noyes*

*O is for . . .*

## *Incy Wincy*

Incy Wincy Spider,
By the classroom sink,
Scared all the children
Who came to get a drink.

Incy Wincy Spider,
Lurking in the drawer,
When the teacher opened it
She fainted on the floor.

Incy Wincy Spider,
Jumped down on the Head,
Now he's hiding in his cupboard,
'I won't come out,' he said.

Incy saw inspectors,
Writing their report,
Climbed up inside their trousers –
They cut their visit short.

Incy Wincy Spider,
In the teachers' loo,
They're too scared to go in there,
What can they do?

Ena cleaned the corner,
Where Incy's cobweb hangs,
Got bitten on the backside
By Incy's monstrous fangs.

Incy Wincy Spider
Has only got one rule,
We all must remember,
A SPIDER RUNS THIS SCHOOL!

*David Orme*

## Gran Can You Rap?

Gran was in her chair she was taking a nap
When I tapped her on the shoulder to see if she could rap.
Gran can you rap? Can you rap? Can you Gran?
And she opened one eye and she said to me, Man,
   I'm the best rapping Gran this world's ever seen
   I'm a tip-top, slip-slap, rap-rap queen.

And she rose from her chair in the corner of the room
And she started to rap with a bim-bam-boom,
And she rolled up her eyes and she rolled round her head
And as she rolled by this is what she said,
   I'm the best rapping Gran this world's ever seen
   I'm a nip-nap, yip-yap, rap-rap queen.

Then she rapped past my dad and she rapped past my
      mother,
She rapped past me and my little baby brother.
She rapped her arms narrow she rapped her arms wide,
She rapped through the door and she rapped outside.
   She's the best rapping Gran this world's ever seen
   She's a drip-drop, trip-trap, rap-rap queen.


She rapped down the garden she rapped down the street,
The neighbours all cheered and they tapped their feet.
She rapped through the traffic lights as they turned red
As she rapped round the corner this is what she said,
   I'm the best rapping Gran this world's ever seen
   I'm a flip-flop, hip-hop, rap-rap queen.


She rapped down the lane she rapped up the hill,
And as she disappeared she was rapping still.
I could hear Gran's voice saying, Listen Man,
Listen to the rapping of the rap-rap Gran.
   I'm the best rapping Gran this world's ever seen
   I'm a –
      tip-top, slip-slap,
         nip-nap, yip-yap,
            hip-hop, trip-trap,
               touch yer cap,
               take a nap,
                  happy, happy, happy, happy,
                     rap ⸺ rap ⸺ queen.

                                          *Jack Ousbey*

                          217

## *Jemima*

Running down the garden path
Jemima seven years old
Lifts her eyes to watch the sun
Drown in clouds of gold.
Sees her old friend smiling down
Through the chestnut tree
Her face among the branches smiles
White as ivory.
Jemima tells her secrets
Her breath is like a sigh
Wishing on a star that falls
Dying through the sky.
Jemima up the evening path
Through twilight bright as noon
Tells anyone who'll listen
'I've been talking to the moon.'

*Gareth Owen*

## *Futility*

Move him into the sun
Gently its touch awoke him once,
At home, whispering of fields unsown.
Always it woke him, even in France,
Until this morning and this snow.
If anything might rouse him now
The kind old sun will know.

Think how it wakes the seeds
Woke once the clays of a cold star.
Are limbs, so dear-achieved, are sides
Full-nerved, still warm, too hard to stir?
Was it for this the clay grew tall?
O what made fatuous sunbeams toil
To break earth's sleep at all?

*Wilfred Owen*

# *P is for . . .*

## Reading the Classics

The Secret Garden will never age;
The tangled undergrowth remains as fresh
As when the author put down her pen.
Its mysteries are as poignant now as then.

Though Time's a thief it cannot thieve
One page from the world of make-believe.

On the track the Railway Children wait;
Alice still goes back and forth through the glass;
In Tom's Midnight Garden Time unfurls,
And children still discover secret worlds.

At the Gates of Dawn Pan plays his pipes;
Mole and Ratty still float in awe downstream.
The weasels watch, hidden in the grass.
None cares how quickly human years pass.

Though Time's a thief it cannot thieve
One page from the world of make-believe.

*Brian Patten*

## *Waltzing Matilda*

Once a jolly swagman camped by a billabong
    Under the shade of a coolibah tree,
And he sang as he watched and waited till his billy boiled,
    'You'll come a-waltzing Matilda with me!'
Waltzing Matilda, waltzing Matilda,
    You'll come a-waltzing Matilda with me:
And he sang as he watched and waited till his billy boiled,
    'You'll come a-waltzing Matilda with me!'

Down came a jumbuck to drink at the billabong,
    Up jumped the swagman and grabbed him with glee,
And he sang as he stowed that jumbuck in his tucker bag,
    'You'll come a-waltzing Matilda with me!'
Waltzing Matilda, waltzing Matilda
    You'll come a-waltzing Matilda with me:
And he sang as he stowed that jumbuck in his tucker bag,
    'You'll come a-waltzing Matilda with me!'

Up rode the squatter mounted on his thoroughbred,
    Up rode the troopers, one, two, three.
'Where's that jolly jumbuck you've got in your tucker bag?
    You'll come a-waltzing Matilda with me!'
Waltzing Matilda, waltzing Matilda,
    You'll come a-waltzing Matilda with me:
'Where's that jolly jumbuck you've got in your tucker bag?
    You'll come a-waltzing Matilda with me!'

Up jumped the swagman and sprang into the billabong,
  'You'll never take me alive!' said he.
And his ghost may be heard as you pass by that billabong,
  'You'll never take me alive!' said he.
Waltzing Matilda, waltzing Matilda,
  You'll come a-waltzing Matilda with me,
And his ghost may be heard as you pass by that billabong,
  'You'll come a-waltzing Matilda with me!'

*Andrew Barton 'Banjo' Paterson*

## Some Aunts and Uncles

When Aunty Jane
Became a Crane
She put one leg behind her head;
And even when the clock struck ten
Refused to go to bed.

When Aunty Grace
Became a Plaice
She all but vanished sideways on;
Except her nose
And pointed toes
The rest of her was gone.

When Aunty Flo
Became a Crow
She had a bed put in a tree;
And there she lay
And read all day
Of ornithology.

When Aunty Vi
Became a Fly
Her favourite nephew
Sought her life;
How could he know
That with each blow
He bruised his Uncle's wife?

When Aunty Mig
Became a Pig
She floated on the briny breeze,
With irritation in her heart
And warts upon her knees.

When Uncle Jake
Became a Snake
He never found it out;
And so as no one mentions it
One sees him still about.

*Mervyn Peake*

# Last Night I Saw the City Breathing

Last night, I saw the City breathing:
Great Gusts of people,
Rushing in and
Puffing out
Of Stations' singing mouths

Last night, I saw the City laughing.
Take-Aways got the giggles,
Cinemas split their sides,
And Living Rooms completely creased themselves!

Last night, I saw the City dancing.
Shadows were cheek to cheek with brick walls,
Trains wiggled their hips all over the place,
And the trees
In the breeze
Put on a show for an audience of windows!

Last night, I saw the city starving,
Snaking Avenue smacked her lips
And swallowed seven roundabouts!
Fat office blocks got stuffed with light
And gloated over empty parking lots.

Last night, I saw the City crying.
Cracked windows poured falling stars
And the streets were paved with mirrors.

Last night, I saw the City sit down at last.
Armchairs cuddled up to warm human beings
And a million cups of tea
Made best friends with a million pairs of hands.

Last night, I saw the City sleeping.
Roads night-dreamed,
Street Lamps quietly boasted,
'When I grow up, I'm going to be a star!'
And the Wind,
Like a cat,
Snoozed in the nooks of roofs.

*Andrew Fusek Peters*

## Cousin Autumn

Summer packed her bags today
To take her annual holiday
She jetted off beyond our reach
To seek the perfect golden beach.
She left a cousin in her place,
A cheeky chap with ruddy face.
We saw him bring a paintbox too,
But didn't know what he would do.
You see, this strange, eccentric fellow
Is daubing trees in red and yellow.

*Polly Peters*

## The Way I Am

I'm just an ordinary sort of boy,
Not the centre of attention,
The best of the bunch,
Apple of the teacher's eye,
The one everyone remembers.
**IT'S JUST THE WAY I AM.**

I'm just an ordinary sort of boy,
Not the high flier,
Captain of the team,
Star of the school play,
Top of the class.
**IT'S JUST THE WAY I AM.**

I'm just an ordinary sort of boy,
Nothing special at all,
Run of the mill,
Fair to middling,
No great shakes.
**IT'S JUST THE WAY I AM.**

I'm just an ordinary sort of boy,
But I'm not invisible.
I do exist!
I'm as different as anyone else,
There's nobody like me.
And to my family, I'm pretty special.

So please, Sir, please, Miss – notice ME sometimes.
**I AM WHAT I AM.**

*Gervase Phinn*

## *Jingle Bells*

Dashing through the snow,
In a one-horse open sleigh;
O'er the fields we go,
Laughing all the way;
Bells on bob-tail ring,
Making spirits bright;
Oh what fun to ride and sing
A sleighing song tonight.

Jingle bells, jingle bells,
Jingle all the way;
Oh! What joy it is to ride
In a one-horse open sleigh.
Jingle bells, jingle bells,
Jingle all the way;
Oh! What joy it is to ride
In a one-horse open sleigh.

*James Pierpont*

## *Marshmallow*

Pink ones
White ones
Pink ones
White ones
Pink ones
White ones
Green ones

Eh?

*Simon Pitt*

## Extract from *The Bed Book*

Beds come in all sizes –
Single or double,
Cot-size or cradle,
King-size or trundle.

Most Beds are Beds
For sleeping or resting,
But the *best* Beds are much
More interesting!

Not just a white little
Tucked-in-tight little
Nighty-night little
Turn-out-the-light little
Bed —

Instead
A Bed for Fishing,
A Bed for Cats,
A Bed for a Troupe of
Acrobats.

The *right* sort of Bed
(If you see what I mean)
Is a Bed that might
Be a Submarine

Nosing through water
Clear and green,
Silver and glittery
As a sardine

Or a Jet-Propelled Bed
For visiting Mars
With mosquito nets
For the shooting stars . . .

*Sylvia Plath*

## Eldorado

Gaily bedight,
A gallant knight,
In sunshine and in shadow,
Had journeyed long,
Singing a song,
In search of Eldorado.

But he grew old –
This knight so bold –
And o'er his heart a shadow
Fell as he found
No spot of ground
That looked like Eldorado.

And, as his strength
Failed him at length,
He met a pilgrim shadow:
'Shadow,' said he,
'Where can it be,
This land of Eldorado?'

'Over the mountains
Of the Moon,
Down the valley of the Shadow,
Ride, boldly ride,'
The shade replied,
'If you seek for Eldorado.'

*Edgar Allan Poe*

## The Quiet Life

Happy the man, whose wish and care
A few paternal acres bound,
Content to breathe his native air
   In his own ground.

Whose herds with milk, whose fields with bread,
Whose flocks supply him with attire;
Whose trees in summer yield him shade,
   In winter, fire.

Blest, who can unconcern'dly find
Hours, days, and years, slide soft away
In health of body, peace of mind,
   Quiet by day.

Sound sleep by night; study and ease
Together mix'd; sweet recreation,
And innocence, which most does please
   With meditation.

Thus let me live, unseen, unknown;
Thus unlamented let me die;
Steal from the world, and not a stone
   Tell where I lie.

*Alexander Pope*

## Why Do I Have to Clean My Room?

Why do I have to clean my room
when I would rather play?
The crayons scattered on the floor
are hardly in the way.
I almost never trip upon
my basketball or drums,
and I don't pay attention
to the cake and cookie crumbs.

Why do I have to clean my room?
I think my room looks nice.
There's pizza in the corner,
but it's only half a slice.
I'm not at all concerned about
the gravy on the chair,
my piles of model planes and trains,
my stacks of underwear.

I will admit some bits of clay
are sticking to the wall.
I scarcely even notice them
and do not mind at all.
Beneath my bed there's just a wedge
of last week's apple pie,
and yet I have to clean my room . . .
I simply don't know why.

*Jack Prelutsky*

## Worms Make Me Squirm

I'm not afraid of spiders
or snakes or mice;
and I think that frogs and snails
are really rather nice.
Earwigs and woodlice I can handle with ease
and I'm fascinated by the bugs and beetles
that live under the trees.
With cockroaches and caterpillars
I can be very bold,
whilst really slimy slugs I love to hold.

But there's one thing in the garden
that I cannot go near;
one thing in the garden
that makes me go all queer.
There's one thing in the garden
that makes me squeal and squirm.
So please
**Please**
**Please**
don't ask me
to pick up a worm!

*Alan Priestley*

## But Of Course There Was Nobody There!

Just when I thought they'd all gone
and I'd sat down to read a good book,
there was a loud creak on the landing
and I dashed up to take a look.

But of course there was nobody there.

Settled once more in my chair
reading a poem about a twin lamb,
I nearly jumped out of my skin
when I heard the kitchen door slam.

But of course there was nobody there!

There came a sort of a groan
from the back of the house somewhere.
Then shocked by the shrill of the phone
I picked it up and answered with care.

But of course there was nobody there.

My nerves were now torn to shreds.
My heart was beating much faster.
I wished I was not on my own –
the day was a total disaster.

But of course there was nobody there.

Now frightened and ready to scream
I buried my head in my arms,
only to be roused from my terror
when the door bell rang like an alarm.

Would there be somebody there?

Scared and dripping with sweat
I went and opened the door.
Outside on the step lay a card
saying 'I rang till my finger was sore –

But there seemed to be no one there.'

I looked at myself in a mirror
And was startled by what I saw
There was absolutely no sign of me
I checked the mirror once more,

But I definitely wasn't there!

*Janis Priestley*

# *Q is for . . .*

## A Good-Night

Close now thine eyes, and rest secure;
  Thy soul is safe enough, thy body sure;
  He that loves thee, he that keeps
And guards thee, never slumbers, never sleeps . . .

*Francis Quarles*

*R is for . . .*

## I Wish

I wish I loved the human race,
I wish I loved its silly face,
I wish I loved the way it walks,
I wish I loved the way it talks,
And when I'm introduced to one
I wish I thought 'What jolly fun!'

*Walter Raleigh*

## Darling Andrea

I think you're sweet.
Meet me on the street about six.
I'll be doing skateboard tricks
on the ramp in Stuart Pascoe's garden.
You can stand at the gate and cheer,
but don't come too near.
No girls are allowed in Pascoe's gang.

At half past seven
go down on your bike to the chip shop –
buy me some if you like,
plenty of salt and vinegar.
If it gets dark early
I'll give you a kiss.

PS Please keep quiet about this.

*Irene Rawnsley*

# Bouncy Castle

(Bouncy castle, bouncy castle, *recited with actions*)

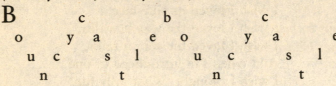

It's my party.
Come and play.

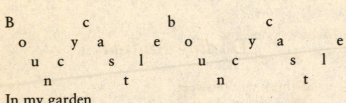

In my garden
for the day.

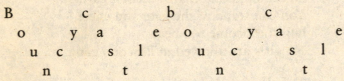

Take your shoes off,
yell and jump.

B   c   b   c
o y a e o y a e
u c s l u c s l
n t n t

Fly up, fall down
with a bump.

B      c        b          c
  o    y  a    e  o     y  a      e
   u  c    s  l    u  c     s  l
    n       t       n         t

Got to beat
that Charlene Brown.

B      c        b          c
  o    y  a    e  o     y  a      e
   u  c    s  l    u  c     s  l
    n       t       n         t

Charlene's gone and
knocked me down.

B      c        b          c
  o    y  a    e  o     y  a      e
   u  c    s  l    u  c     s  l
    n       t       n         t

We're all tangled
in a heap.

B      c        b          c
  o    y  a    e  o     y  a      e
   u  c    s  l    u  c     s  l
    n       t       n         t

Tommy Slater's
gone to sleep.

B     c       b         c
  o    y   a     e   o    y   a      e
   u   c    s   l    u   c    s   l
    n      t       n      t

Time for tea
and birthday cake.

B     c       b         c
  o    y   a     e   o    y   a      e
   u   c    s   l    u   c    s   l
    n      t       n      t

Mum I've got a
jellyache!

B     c       b         c
  o    y   a     e   o    y   a      e
   u   c    s   l    u   c    s   l
    n      t       n      t

Keep on bouncing
till I drop.

B     c       b         c
  o    y   a     e   o    y   a      e
   u   c    s   l    u   c    s   l
    n      t       n      t

Get – ting . . . tired
got . . . to . . . stop.

*Rita Ray*

# *Spells*

I dance and dance without any feet —
This is the spell of the ripening wheat.

With never a tongue I've a tale to tell —
This is the meadow-grasses' spell.

I give you health without any fee —
This is the spell of the apple-tree.

I rhyme and riddle without any book —
This is the spell of the bubbling brook.

Without any legs I run for ever —
This is the spell of the mighty river.

I fall for ever and not at all —
This is the spell of the waterfall.

Without a voice I roar aloud —
This is the spell of the thunder-cloud.

No button or seam has my white coat —
This is the spell of the leaping goat.

I can cheat strangers with never a word —
This is the spell of the cuckoo-bird.

We have tongues in plenty but speak no names –
This is the spell of the fiery flames.

The creaking door has a spell to riddle –
I play a tune without any fiddle.

*James Reeves*

## Careful With That, You Might Break It

See what I've found.

Oh be careful with that,
it's so delicate, it could easily break.

If you take it in your hands gently
you can hold it
close up to your eyes.

It's a bit hazy on the outside,
but if you wait for it to turn,
here and there you can see right through
and then you'll be really amazed!

Gently now, even though it looks solid enough,
you'd be surprised at just how flimsy it is.
Look there. Can you see the big blue bits?
I remember being so fascinated with them
that I wanted to touch them.

But you're not allowed to do that.
If you did, The High says you might damage it
because there's some protective coating
or gas or something surrounding the whole thing
and if that gets damaged, it could be serious.
What do you suppose the green bits are?

That's it, just let it rest in your palm.
Watch how it spins of its own accord.
Have you spotted the brown areas?
No, you mustn't touch the little white thing
going round it, The High says it's very important too,
a force or influence or balance perhaps.
Let's leave it now, careful, don't forget it's so very fragile.

Its name?
The High call it *Earth*.
Some say it's a sad place.

*John Rice*


# When I Came Home on Tuesday

When I came home on tuesday
feeling ever so hungry,
my dad was in the kitchen
making pancakes for our tea.

Into half a pound of flour
he mixed a pint of milk,
cracked eggs into the batter
and beat in smooth as silk.

Next he took the frying pan
and heated drops of oil.
Until the pan was sizzling,
we waited for a while.

Soon everything was ready.
Dad poured batter in the pan
but when we turned it over
   then the fun began.

Dad offered me the frying pan.
'Toss the pancake in the air!'
With both hands on the handle,
   I took my aim with care.

The pancake somersaulted.
It flipped around and round.
When it flopped into the pan,
it had turned up golden brown!

We sat and ate our pancakes,
remembering what it meant.
Tomorrow it's Ash Wednesday,
that's the start of Lent.

*Chris Riley*

## The Sloth

In moving-slow he has no Peer.
You ask him something in his Ear,
He thinks about it for a Year;

And, then, before he says a Word
There, upside down (unlike a Bird),
He will assume that you have Heard –

A most Ex-as-per-at-ing Lug.
But should you call his manner Smug,
He'll sigh and give his Branch a Hug;

Then off again to Sleep he goes,
Still swaying gently by his Toes,
And you just *know* he knows he knows.

*Theodore Roethke*


## For Naomi

I'm the kind of dad
my children don't want to be seen with
because I'm the kind of dad who

shouts in shops
says hello to babies
doesn't clean the car
eats pizzas in the street
doesn't cut his moustache
sings on buses
argues with policemen
waves to old ladies
has long hair
and
writes poems

*Michael Rosen*

## Christmas Daybreak

Before the paling of the stars,
    Before the winter morn,
Before the earliest cockcrow,
    Jesus Christ was born:
Born in a stable,
    Cradled in a manger,
In the world His hands had made,
    Born a stranger.

Priest and king lay fast asleep
   In Jerusalem,
Young and old lay fast asleep
   In crowded Bethlehem:
Saint and angel, ox and ass,
   Kept a watch together,
Before the Christmas daybreak
   In the winter weather.

Jesus on His Mother's breast
   In the stable cold,
Spotless Lamb of God was He,
   Shepherd of the fold.
Let us kneel with Mary Maid,
   With Joseph bent and hoary,
With saint and angel, ox and ass,
   To hail the King of Glory.

*Christina Rossetti*

## Seasoned Cinquains

Autumn
Tinge of henna
Crackling fires and leaves
Deep rooting tick of biding time
Digging.

Winter
Stiff morning air
Cracked ice on sleeping seeds
Frosty breath shiver-shudders words
Waiting.

Spring air
Fairy-wing breeze
Lifting blossom petals
Weightless whispering of summer
Stirring.

Summer
Claiming a crown
Exploding wild colours
In a frenzy of patterning
Clapping.

*Coral Rumble*

*S is for . . .*

## Riddle

From Spain
This golden ball
Is clothed with tangy zest.
It holds the sun
Within its bitter pith
Sunrays ooze sweetness
But also hide a sting.

*Anita Marie Sackett*

## Who Do You Think You Are?

Who do you think you are
and where do you think you came from?
From toenails to the hair of your head you are
    mixed of the earth, of the air,
Of compounds equal to the burning gold and
    amethyst lights of the Mountains of the Blood
    of Christ at Sante Fe.
Listen to the laboratory man tell you what you are
    made of, man, listen while he takes you apart.
Weighing 150 pounds you hold 3,500 cubic feet of
    gas – oxygen, hydrogen, nitrogen.
From the 22 pounds and 10 ounces of carbon in you
    is the filling for 9,000 lead pencils.

In your blood are 50 grains of iron and in the rest of
   your frame enough iron to make a spike that
   would hold your weight.

From your 50 ounces of phosphorus could be made
   800,000 matches and elsewhere in your
   physical premises are hidden 60 lumps of sugar,
   20 teaspoons of salt, 38 quarts of water, two
   ounces of lime, and scatterings of starch,
   chloride of potash, magnesium, sulphur,
   hydrochloric acid.
You are a walking drug store and also a cosmos and a
   phantasmagoria treading a lonesome valley, one
   of the people, one of the minions and
   myrmidons who would like an answer to the
   question, 'Who and what are you?'

*Carl Sandburg*

## *Everyone Sang*

Everyone suddenly burst out singing;
And I was filled with such delight
As prisoned birds must find in freedom,
Winging wildly across the white
Orchards and dark-green fields; on – on – and out of sight.

Everyone's voice was suddenly lifted;
And beauty came like the setting sun:
My heart was shaken with tears; and horror
Drifted away . . . O, but Everyone
Was a bird; and the song was wordless; the singing will
    never be done.

*April 1919*
*Siegfried Sassoon*

## The Apple-Raid

Darkness came early, though not yet cold;
Stars were strung on the telegraph wires;
Street lamps spilled pools of liquid gold;
The breeze was spiced with garden fires.

That smell of burnt leaves, the early dark,
Can still excite me but not as it did
So long ago when we met in the park –
Myself, John Peters and David Kidd.

We moved out of town to the district where
The lucky and wealthy had their homes
With garages, gardens, and apples to spare
Clustered in the trees' green domes.

We chose the place we meant to plunder
And climbed the wall and tip-toed through
The secret dark. Apples crunched under
Our feet as we moved through the grass and dew.

We found the lower boughs of a tree
That were easy to reach. We stored the fruit
In pockets and jerseys until all three
Boys were heavy with their tasty loot.

Safe on the other side of the wall
We moved back to town and munched as we went.
I wonder if David remembers at all
That little adventure, the apples' fresh scent.

Strange to think that he's fifty years old,
That tough little boy with scabs on his knees;
Stranger to think that John Peters lies cold
In an orchard in France beneath apple trees.

*Vernon Scannell*

## The Gallant Ship

Upon the gale she stooped her side,
And bounded o'er the swelling tide,
    As she were dancing home;
The merry seamen laughed to see
Their gallant ship so lustily
    Furrow the sea-green foam.

*Sir Walter Scott*

## Encounter

One spring evening I came home
smelling of chalk and felt tips
and saw him: lager-pale, eyes
bright in the headlamps.

I thought of farmers, but my heart
was on his side. I would have loved,
like a woman to a cat, to talk to him.
But he retreated, a shy child

from a stranger, down the bank,
into gorse, brambles and dog roses.
I remembered Lawrence's snake
as he'd remembered the albatross.

But my heart was lighter
when I turned the key in the lock.
I imagined smells of sandy soil,
gorse, cold spring air, and fox.

*Fred Sedgwick*


## Crabbèd Age and Youth

Crabbèd Age and Youth
Cannot live together:
Youth is full of pleasance,
Age is full of care;
Youth like summer morn,
Age like winter weather;
Youth like summer brave,
Age like winter bare.
Youth is full of sport,
Age's breath is short;
Youth is nimble, Age is lame;
Youth is hot and bold,
Age is weak and cold;
Youth is wild, and Age is tame.
Age, I do abhor thee;
Youth, I do adore thee;
O, my Love, my Love is young!

Age, I do defy thee:
O, sweet shepherd, hie thee!
For methinks thou stay'st too long.

*William Shakespeare (attrib.)*

## *How to Successfully Persuade Your Parents to Give You More Pocket Money*

Ask, request, demand, suggest, cajole or charm
Ingratiate, suck up to, flatter, compliment or smarm
Negotiate, debate, discuss, persuade, convince, explain
Or reason, justify, protest, object, dispute, complain
Propose, entreat, beseech, beg, plead, appeal, implore
Harass, go on about it, pester, winge, whine, nag and bore
Annoy, insult, reproach, denounce, squeal, scream and
  shout
Go quiet, subdued, look worried, fret, brood, tremble,
  shiver, pout

Act depressed, downhearted, upset, snivel, sigh
Go all glum and plaintive, wobble bottom lip and cry
Sniff, sulk, grumble, stare at ceiling, mope, pine, stay in
  bed

Get cross, get angry, fume, seethe, fester, agitate, see red
Provoke, enrage, push, bully, aggravate and goad
Screech, smoke, burn up, ignite, spark, detonate,
  EXPLODE

And if all that doesn't work

Here are two little tricks
That should do it with ease

No. 1: smile
No. 2: say please.

*Andrea Shavick*

# Song

A widow bird sate mourning for her love
    Upon a wintry bough;
The frozen wind crept on above,
    The freezing stream below.

There was no leaf upon the forest bare,
    No flower upon the ground,
And little motion in the air
    Except the mill-wheel's sound.

*Percy Bysshe Shelley*

## A Card for Mother's Day

You're cuddlier than a nettle,
kinder than a great white shark,
jollier than a graveyard
at midnight in the dark,

calmer than a thunderstorm,
neater than sloshy mud,
more elegant than a hippo
or a cow that's chewing cud,

lovelier than a potato,
gentler than an avalanche,
more charming than a squawking crow
squatting on its branch,

livelier than a bathroom sponge,
warmer than Arctic ice,
more generous than a teaspoon
with a single grain of rice,

softer than a ball and chain,
wiser than a wooden plank,
because today is Mother's Day
it's you I have to thank

for everything you've done for me,
for keeping me in your clutch,
you're sweeter than lime pickle
and I love you very much.

*Norman Silver*

## Hector the Collector

Hector the Collector
Collected bits of string,
Collected dolls with broken heads
And rusty bells that would not ring.
Pieces out of picture puzzles,
Bent-up nails and ice-cream sticks,
Twists of wires, worn-out tyres,
Paper bags and broken bricks.
Old chipped vases, half shoelaces,
Gatlin' guns that wouldn't shoot,
Leaky boats that wouldn't float
And stopped-up horns that wouldn't toot.
Butter knives that had no handles,
Copper keys that fit no locks,
Rings that were too small for fingers,
Dried-up leaves and patched-up socks.
Worn-out belts that had no buckles,
'Lectric trains that had no tracks,
Airplane models, broken bottles,

Three-legged chairs and cups with cracks.
Hector the Collector
Loved these things with all his soul –
Loved them more than shining diamonds,
Loved them more than glistenin' gold.
Hector called to all the people,
'Come and share my treasure trunk!'
And all the silly sightless people
Came and looked . . . and called it junk.

*Shel Silverstein*


## How Do You Say Goodbye?

How do you say goodbye to a house
when you're moving forever on Saturday,
When you've lived there always – seven years,
And no matter what, they won't let you stay?

How do you say goodbye to a room
With its just-right walls and corners and nooks,
With its Snoopy curtains, all faded and blue,
And shelves for your toys, and fishtank, and books?

How do you say goodbye to the tree
That grew up so tall by your bedroom window,
That dances its leaves on your yellow walls
And lulls you to sleep whenever the wind blows?

How do you say goodbye to a street
Where you know all the hedges and places to hide,
The back-alley fence where you broke your arm,
And the hill at the end where you used to slide?

I wish I could move this house and this tree –
This year – this street – these swings;
My friends can all come and visit me,
But how do you say goodbye to things?

*Lois Simmie*

## Nature's Paintbox

Blue in Spring is a pastel blue,
In Autumn blue is bold,
Summer's blue's heart-warming,
Winter's is ice-cold.

White in Spring is brand-new lambs,
In Autumn white goes grey,
Summer's white's an ice-cream white,
Winter's snow all day!

Spring's red's a bunch of tulips
Autumn's the fading rose,
Summer's red is sunburnt skin,
Winter's a raw and sniffly nose.

270

Winter's yellow's cough syrup,
Summer's is suns that laugh,
Autumn's the turning of the leaf,
In Spring it's crocus and daff.

Spring's favourite colour is green,
Autumn's favourite's brown,
Summer warms the colours up,
Winter cools them down.

*Matt Simpson*

## My Dad's Amazing!

My dad's **amazing** for he can:

make mountains out of molehills,
teach Granny to suck eggs,
make Mum's blood boil
and then drive her up the wall.

My dad's **amazing** for he also:

walks around with his head in the clouds,
has my sister eating out of his hand,
says he's got eyes in the back of his head
and can read me like a book.

But, the most **amazing** thing of all is:

when he's caught someone red-handed,
first he jumps down their throat
and then he bites their head off!

*Ian Souter*

## Chalk

As we walk across this hill of chalk
It's hard to imagine
That once these hills
Were below the sea
Chalk is the sediment
Left by a million tiny creatures
On the seabed
I think of that
As we walk upon this thin skin
Of earth and grass
Beneath the blue sky
And a burning sun

*Roger Stevens*

## Block City

What are you able to build with your blocks?
Castles and palaces, temples and docks.
Rain may keep raining, and others go roam,
But I can be happy and building at home.

Let the sofa be mountains, the carpet be sea,
There I'll establish a city for me:
A kirk and a mill and a palace beside,
And a harbour as well where my vessels may ride.

Great is the palace with pillar and wall,
A sort of a tower on top of it all,
And steps coming down in an orderly way
To where my toy vessels lie safe in the bay.

This one is sailing and that one is moored:
Hark to the song of the sailors on board!
And see on the steps of my palace, the kings
Coming and going with presents and things!

Now that I have done with it, down let it go!
All in a moment the town is laid low.
Block upon block lying scattered and free,
What is there left of my town by the sea?

Yet as I saw it, I see it again,
The kirk and the palace, the ships and the men,
And as long as I live and where'er I may be,
I'll always remember my town by the sea.

*Robert Louis Stevenson*

## Sir, Say No More

Sir, say no more.
Within me 't is as if
The green and climbing eyesight of a cat
Crawled near my mind's poor birds.

*Trumbull Stickney*

## Game's End

On autumn evenings the children still play in the park,
Scuffing up the sweet-smelling aftermath,
Their shadows in the sunset triple length,
Making heroic kicks, half-legendary saves:
They play until it is dark,
And still for a little while after can be seen
By the flitting of their plimsolls, by their sleeves,
And by the twinkling orb of grass-stained polythene
Rising up white against dark sky or leaves.

Till, by some common consent, the game must close.
No one bothers any more to yell 'Pass' or 'Shoot',
Someone gives the ball a last terrific boot
Into the air and before it falls they are gone,
Wheeling away over the grass,
Snatching their sweaters up for the goalposts, going
Who knows where, only later to see how soon
The white ball never fell, but went on climbing
Into the dark air, and became the moon.

*David Sutton*

## All the Dogs

You should have seen him –
he stood in the park and whistled,
underneath an oak tree,
and all the dogs came bounding up
and sat around him,
keeping their big eyes on him,
tails going like pendulums.
And there was one cocker pup
who went and licked his hand,
and a Labrador who whimpered
till the rest joined in.

Then he whistled a second time,
high-pitched as a stoat,
over all the shouted dog names
and whistles of owners,
till a flurry of paws
brought more dogs, panting,
as if they'd come miles,
and these too found space
on the flattened grass
to stare at the boy's
unmemorable face
which all the dogs found special.

*Matthew Sweeney*

## A Question of Scale

So, naturalists observe, a flea
Hath smaller fleas that on him prey;
And these have smaller fleas to bite 'em,
And so proceed *ad infinitum*.

*Jonathan Swift*

## Cracks in the Pavement

Those cracks in the pavement,
as everyone knows,
mustn't be stepped on.
Not even a toe
should venture to try it.
Don't laugh, it's quite true.
Let me tell you the story
of Brian McGrew
who jumped on a crack
with an 'I don't care' grin.
At once, the crack opened.
The boy was dragged in
by a large, scaly hand.
He had time for one shriek,
then vanished entirely.
Gone for a week,
he was found in Australia,
mad as a hatter.
So don't say that avoiding
the cracks doesn't matter.
Just hop, skip and jump,
that's all you need do,
while remembering the story
of Brian McGrew.

*Marian Swinger*

## A Small Girl Swinging

When first they pushed me
    I was very scared.
My tummy jiggled. I was
    Unprepared.

The second time was higher
    And my ears
Were cold with whisperings
    Of tiny fears.

The third time up was HIGH,
    My teeth on edge.
My heart leapt off the bedroom
    Window ledge.

The fourth time, Oh, the fourth time
    It was mad.
My shirt flew off the world
    And I was glad.

No one's pushing now,
    My ears are ringing.
Who'll see across the park
    A small girl swinging?

Who'll hear across the park
   Her mother calling,
And everywhere her shadows
   Rising, falling?

*George Szirtes*

*T is for . . .*

## Ozone Friendly Poem

It won't damage the EARTH,
or pollute the sea
It won't psych your mind
neither poison your body
these words have power
when used properly.
Because
This poem is OZONE FRIENDLY.

Words can be creative
words can sound great
we can use words to instruct
and to communicate,
these words are not destructive
violating a tree.
Because
This poem is OZONE FRIENDLY.

My words take shape
they are organized
they won't burn the EARTH'S skin
like pesticides
they're not manufactured using CFCs.
Because
This poem is OZONE FRIENDLY.

Digest these words
feel positive
don't panic, get stressed
they're free from additives,
you won't regurgitate them
like smoke from a factory.
Because
This poem is OZONE FRIENDLY.

These words are SAFE
I can testify
they won't destroy the OZONE LAYER
beyond the sky,
you can analyse this poem
in a laboratory.
You'll find
This poem is OZONE FRIENDLY.

Recycle, regenerate
don't waste energy
conservation of the EARTH
is just a part of the key
and I'll keep on using these words
well naturally.
You see
This poem is OZONE FRIENDLY.

*Levi Tafari*

## Hill Rolling

I kind of exploded inside,
and joy shot out of me.
I began my roll down the grassy hill.
I bent my knees up small, took a deep breath
And I was off.
My arms shot out sideways.
I gathered speed.
My eyes squinted.
Sky and grass, dazzle and dark.

I went on for ever,
My arms were covered with dents,
holes, squashed grass.
Before I knew it I was at the bottom.
The game was over,
The door of the classroom closed behind me.
I can smell chalk dust, and hear the voice of teacher,
to make me forget my hill

*Andrew Taylor*

## Today I Saw the Dragon-fly

Today I saw the dragon-fly
Come from the wells where he did lie.

An inner impulse rent the veil
Of his old husk: from head to tail
Came out clear plates of sapphire mail.
He dried his wings: like gauze they grew;
Through crofts and pastures wet with dew
A living flash of light he flew.

*Alfred, Lord Tennyson*


## The Song of the Mischievous Dog

There are many who say that a dog has its day,
  And a cat has a number of lives;
There are others who think that a lobster is pink,
  And that bees never work in their hives.
There are fewer, of course, who insist that a horse
  Has a horn and two humps on its head,
And a fellow who jests that a mare can build nests
  Is as rare as a donkey that's red.
Yet in spite of all this, I have moments of bliss,
  For I cherish a passion for bones,
And though doubtful of biscuit, I'm willing to risk it,

And I love to chase rabbits and stones.
But my greatest delight is to take a good bite
At a calf that is plump and delicious;
And if I indulge in a bite at a bulge,
Let's hope you won't think me too vicious.

*Dylan Thomas*

## Thaw

Over the land freckled with snow half-thawed
The speculating rooks at their nests cawed
And saw from elm-tops, delicate as flower of grass,
What we below could not see, Winter pass.

*Edward Thomas*

## Dragons Are Back

Alas, alack
The dragons are back
And any time now
They're bound to attack.
The sky will turn
From blue to black
With lightning-flash
And thunder-crack.

The dragons are back
The dragons are back
The dragons, the dragons
The dragons are back.

They snap their jaws
Snickerty-snack,
Flash their claws
Flickerty-flack,
Twitch their tails
Thwickerty thwack,
Clank their scales
Clickerty-clack.

The dragons are back
The dragons are back
The dragons, the dragons
The dragons are back.

The mill goes still.
The wind is slack.
The cows won't milk.
The ducks don't quack.
We try to talk
But just lose track:
Go mumble jumble
Yakkity-yak.

The dragons are back
The dragons are back
The dragons, the dragons
The dragons are back.

We dare not stay.
We quickly pack.
But every road's
A cul-de-sac.
The priest has had
A heart attack.
The king's become
A maniac.

The dragons are back
The dragons are back
The dragons, the dragons
The dragons are back.

*Nick Toczek*


## Cat

The fat cat on the mat
may seem to dream
of nice mice that suffice
for him, or cream;
but free, maybe,
walks in thought
unbowed, proud, where loud
roared and fought
his kin, lean and slim,
or deep in den
in the East feasted on beasts
and tender men.

The giant lion with iron
claw in paw,
and huge ruthless tooth
in gory jaw;
the pard dark-starred
fleet upon feet
that oft soft from aloft
leaps on his meat
where woods loom in gloom –
far now they be,
fierce and free,
and tamed is he;
but fat cat on the mat
kept as a pet,
he does not forget.

*J. R. R. Tolkien*

## The New Generation

Wizards look like everyday folk
despite what you've been told.
We don't have long white whiskers
nor are we very old.

We don't go round in trailing robes
except on special days;
those pointed hats are stylish
but out of the usual way.

We don't wear silver stars and moons
embroidered on our clothes;
we never wear those pointy shoes
they're murder on the toes.

I like to wear my Levi's,
roar up and down the street
on my Ducatti motorbike,
Doc Martens on my feet.

I'm part of a new generation
of wizard girls, we're cool!
No one dares to mess with me
Female wizards rule!

*Angela Topping*

## Fox Shopping

Dustbins done.
Drained the drains.
Chicken house checked –
bother those chains.
Bird scraps snatched.
Not much here.
How I hate
this time of year.

*Jill Townsend*

## *Batman*

Batman
Age 10½
Patrols the streets of his suburb
At night
Between 7 and 8 o'clock.
If he is out later than this
he is spanked
and sent to bed
Without supper.

Batman
Almost 11
Patrols the streets of his suburb
At night
If he has finished his homework.

Batman,
His secret identity
And freckles
Protected
By the mask and cloak
His Auntie Elsie
Made on her sewing machine,
Patrols
At night
Righting Wrongs.

Tonight he is on the trail of
Raymond age 11
(large for his age)
Who has stolen Stephen's
Gobstoppers and football cards.

Batman
Patrolling the streets of his suburb
Righting Wrongs
Finds Raymond,
Demands the return of the stolen goods.
Raymond knocks him over,
Rips his mask,
Tears his cloak,
And steals his utility belt.
Batman starts to cry,
Wipes his eyes with his cape
(His hankie was in the belt).

Next day
Auntie Elsie says
This is the fourteenth time
I've had to mend your
Batman costume.
If it happens again
You'll have to whistle for it.

Batman
Eats a bag of crisps.

*John Turner*

## In My Day

In my day
we got up at dawn,
made our own beds,
cooked our breakfasts,
walked to school,
worked hard,
didn't talk in class,
walked home,
enjoyed our homework,
ate all our food,
washed our plates
and went to bed early.
And told lies.

*Steve Turner*

# U *is for . . .*

## An Alien Ate My Homework

An Alien ate my homework.
I assure you, Miss, it's true.
I know you think I'm fibbing, Miss,
But would I lie to you?

I'll tell you how it happened, Miss,
I was alone last night.
I'd finished all my sums, Miss.
Yes, I *know* I got them right.

I was writing up my science
Which, quite frankly, Miss, was hard –
When a spaceship came and hovered
In the air above my yard!

A door slid slowly open, Miss,
And to my great surprise
I found myself regarded
By a pair of purple eyes.

The thing was green, with tentacles.
My heart was filled with fear.
I knew it wanted something,
But quite what, I wasn't clear.

Until it ate my homework, Miss!
Just snatched it clean away!
And then – what's that you're saying, Miss?
Detention, Miss? OK.

*Kaye Umansky*

## Questions at Night

Why
Is the sky?

What starts the thunder overhead?
Who makes the crashing noise?
Are the angels falling out of bed?
Are they breaking all their toys?

Why does the sun go down so soon?
Why do the night-clouds crawl
Hungrily up to the new-laid moon
And swallow it, shell and all?

If there's a Bear among the stars,
As all the people say,
Won't he jump over those pasture-bars
And drink up the Milky Way?

Does every star that happens to fall
Turn into a firefly?
Can't it ever get back to Heaven at all?
And why
Is the sky?

Louis Untermeyer

## January

The days are short,
The sun a spark
Hung thin between
The dark and dark.

Fat snowy footsteps
Track the floor,
And parkas pile up
Near the door.

The river is
A frozen place
Held still beneath
The trees' black lace.

The sky is low.
　　The wind is grey.
The radiator
　　Purrs all day.

*John Updike*

## I Love Thee, Flowers

I love thee, flowers
I love thee, trees
Thine odours drift upon the breeze
My nostrils to refill

But the reeds
And pungent fronds
Decaying in the stagnant ponds
Doth cause me to feel ill

*Ursula Urquhart*

# V *is for* . . .

## Eternity

I saw Eternity the other night
Like a great Ring of pure and endless light,
   All calm, as it was bright;
And round beneath it, Time in hours, days, years,
   Driven by the spheres
Like a vast shadow moved, in which the world
   And all her train were hurled.

*Henry Vaughan*

## Sweet Suffolk Owl

Sweet Suffolk Owl, so trimly dight
With feathers, like a lady bright,
Thou sing'st alone, sitting by night,
   *Te whit! Te whoo! Te whit! To whit!*

Thy note that forth so freely rolls
With shrill command the mouse controls;
And sings a dirge for dying souls –
   *Te whit! Te whoo! Te whit! To whit!*

*Thomas Vautor*

## *Harvey*

Harvey doesn't laugh about how I stay short
   while everybody grows.
Harvey remembers I like jellybeans – except black.
Harvey lends me shirts I don't have to give back.
I'm scared of ghosts and only Harvey knows.

Harvey thinks I will when I say someday I will
   marry Margie Rose.
Harvey shares his lemonade – sip for sip.
He whispers 'zip' when I forget to zip.
He swears I don't have funny-looking toes.

Harvey calls me up when I'm in bed with a sore
   throat and runny nose.
Harvey says I'm nice – but not *too* nice.
And if there is a train to Paradise,
I won't get on it unless Harvey goes.

*Judith Viorst*

## For a Little Love

For a little love, I would go to the end of the world
I would go with my head bare and feet unshod
I would go through ice, but in my soul forever May,
I would go through the storm, but still hear the blackbird
  sing
I would go through the desert, and have pearls of dew in
  my heart.
For a little love, I would go to the end of the world,
Like the one who sings at the door and begs.

*Jaroslav Vrchlicky,*
*translated from the Czech by*
*Vera Fusek Peters and Andrew Fusek Peters*

*W is for . . .*

# The Story of My Life
### List of Discontents

The times, so far, this week
That I've been finger wagged and grounded . . . . . . . . . . 2

The times, today, to tidy
I've been hassled and been hounded . . . . . . . . . . . . . . . . 4

The number of maths homeworks
I've to do by MONDAY NEXT . . . . . . . . . . . . . . . . . . . . 4

The stack of *Thank You* letters
I MUST handwrite – and NOT text! . . . . . . . . . . . . . . . 10

The weeks of pocket money
For dad's heirloom that I broke . . . . . . . . . . . . . . . . . . 12

The number of apologies –
Can't adults take a joke? . . . . . . . . . . . . . . . . . . . . . . . 12

The tests I've had this term
When I've come bottom of my stream . . . . . . . . . . . . . . 12

The matches played this term
When I've been left out of the team . . . . . . . . . . . . . . . 12

The times that dad and me
Have seen the Rovers thrashed this season . . . . . . . . . 100

The times, so far this year,
When I've been fed up with good reason! . . . . . . . . . 1000

*Philip Waddell*

## My Old Bear

has been in the wars,
has had the stuffing
knocked out of him
long since,
sits hunched
with shrivelled arms,
droops
limp ears,
glares
a single orange eye
like some tetchy colonel.

Given the chance
he could tell
of escapades,
fighting the mumps,
soaking up tears,
getting through exams,
but seems content to rest
on the shelf,
kept in reserve
and not forgotten.

*Barrie Wade*

## Pelican

Pelican, Pelican,
  Why so big a beak?
Is that where the words live
That you would like to speak?
Long words, special words,
Words to keep for best,
Words you've loved forever
Since your egg-days in the nest?

Pelican, Pelican,
  I have words like that,
Safe inside my word-cage
Underneath my hat:
Dodecahedron, sycamore, rose,
Paprika, chameleon,
Words such as those.

Pelican, Pelican,
  Open up your beak,
Share your thesaurus,
I long to hear you speak.
Ungainly and cumbersome,
You're not a pretty bird,
But, Pelican, your name is
My favourite feathered word.

*Celia Warren*

## Heatwave Summer

The summer I was nine
I grew
A white skin bikini
With brown arms and legs
My nose peeled
And I wore
White sand stockings on my wet legs.
Got water up my nose
And sand in the sheets.
Went up and down escalators
(With sore feet)
And tried on a hundred black school shoes all size
one-and-a-half
Ate ice-blocks at teatime
(And grew a pink moustache)
Ate fish and chips in paper.
Kissed half-forgotten uncles
And danced in tingling seas
In a holiday heatwave.

*Cathy Warry*

## *An old plot of land*

Just an old plot of land
At the top of our street,
Where gangsters and cowboys
And soldiers could meet.

Where bonfires were built
And promises made,
Where secrets were kept
And debts were repaid.

Where an old air-raid shelter,
A relic of war,
Still stood strong and smelly
As it had years before.

Where friendships were broken,
A squabble a fight,
Foes before lunch
But we'd made up by night.

Where girlfriends were given
A peck on the cheek,
Where romance would blossom
And end in a week.

Just an old plot of land
I still see through the haze
Of magical memories –
My childhood days.

*Clive Webster*

## Some Stuff in a Sack

One summer's day at half past three
Old Ginger Tom went off to sea,
With some stuff in a sack,
And a parrot called Jack,
Sing Fiddle-dee-fiddle-dee-dee.

Beneath the sun he dozed a while,
Then woke up by a desert isle,
With some stuff in a sack,
Like two boots big and black,
And a parrot called Jack,
Sing Fiddle-dee-fiddle-dee-dee.

He crossed a jungle dark and dim
And nothing seemed to bother him,
With some stuff in a sack,
Like a drum he could whack,
And a parrot called Jack,
Sing Fiddle-dee-fiddle-dee-dee.

He gathered wood beside a lake
And built a fire and took a break,
With some stuff in a sack,
Like a fish finger snack,
And a parrot called Jack,
Sing Fiddle-dee-fiddle-dee-dee.

He met a fearsome pirate crew
But knew exactly what to do,
With some stuff in a sack,
Like a whip that went crack,
And a parrot called Jack,
Sing Fiddle-dee-fiddle-dee-dee.

And then he walked along the shore
And thought he'd put to sea once more,
With some stuff in a sack,
Like a map to get back,
And a parrot called Jack,
Sing Fiddle-dee-fiddle-dee-dee.

And when there came a mighty storm,
Old Ginger Tom slept snug and warm
With some stuff in a sack,
Like a waterproof mac,
And a parrot called Jack,
Sing Fiddle-dee-fiddle-dee-dee.

He woke up when the storm had passed
And saw that he was home at last,
With no stuff in the sack,
(Nothing left to unpack),
Sing Fiddle-dee-fiddle-dee-dee.

And all next day the tale he told
Of Tom's Adventures, Brave and Bold
With some stuff in a sack,
Like two boots big and black,
And a drum he could whack,
And a fish finger snack,
And a whip that went crack,
And a map to get back,
And a waterproof mac,
But that parrot called Jack
Sang: FIDDLE-DEE-FIDDLE-DEE-DEE!

*Colin West*


## ABB.

The world is such a crazy place,
Full of the strange and absurd.
Like why is abbreviation
Such a very long word?

*Chris White*

## *I Think I Could Turn and Live with Animals*

I think I could turn and live with animals, they're so
    placid and self-contained,
I stand and look at them long and long.

They do not sweat and whine about their condition,
They do not lie awake in the dark and weep for their sins,
They do not make me sick discussing their duty to God,
Not one is dissatisfied, not one is demented with the mania
    of owning things,
Not one kneels to another, nor to his kind that lived
    thousands of years ago,
Not one is respectable or unhappy over the whole earth.

*Walt Whitman*

## The Vikings

The Vikings wear their horny hats
And sail their beaky boats.
They plait their hair in yellow plaits,
And stink like billy goats.

A Viking has a bristly beard.
He is a bristly feller.
His folk beliefs are pretty weird.
He carries an umbrella.

His moral life, alas, is lax.
He plunders and he pillages.
He wields a nifty battleaxe
And terrorizes villages

He drinks a lot of lagers
From enormous Viking flagons
He sings a lot of sagas
And he slays a lot of dragons.

Consider his behaviour
Is it not extremely jolly?
He comes from Scandinavia.
I lied about the brolly.

*John Whitworth*

## The Last Steam Train to Margate
*for Allen Rothwell*

Gossssh
I wisssh
I were a busss
It's muccch less work
And muccch less fuss
I ssshould like that
I ssschould like that
I ssschould like that
I SSSCHOULD like that
I ssshould like that
De-deedle-dee
De-diddle-dum
Just look at me
'Cause here I come
Faster and faster
Tickerty-boo, what'll I do?
Tearing along, terribly fast
Singing a song, sounding a blast
Whoo, whoo! Out of the way
Goodness me, I can't delay!
You can relax, I have to run
Follow the tracks into the sun
Pain in my back, aches in my joints
Tickerty-tack, here are the points
Diddly-dee, diddly dee
Diddly WIDDLY diddly dee!

Far to go? Not very far.
Little black tunnel
(Tickerty WHAAAH!)
Look over there. What can it be?
Lucky old you, clever old me
Come all this way, rattling along,
Come every day, singing my song
Down to the seaside. Let's have a cheer!
Oh, what a train-ride. We're nearly there,
We're nearly there, we're nearly there, we're nearly there
And now I'd better slow right down
In half a mile we reach the town
And then you take your buckets and spades
And dig the sand and watch the parades
And sing and paddle and splash in the sea
And have ice cream and jelly for tea
And Coca Cola, orange squassssh
And ginger beer, hooray we're here
But gosssh I'm tired
Oh gosssh I'm tired
Oh gosssh I'm tired
Hohhh
GOSSSSSSSSSSSSSSSHHHHHHHHHHHHH

*Ian Whybrow*

## Symphony in Yellow

An omnibus across the bridge
Crawls like a yellow butterfly,
And, here and there, a passer-by
Shows like a little restless midge.

Big barges full of yellow hay
Are moved against the shadowy wharf,
And, like a yellow silken scarf,
The thick fog hangs along the quay.

The yellow leaves begin to fade
And flutter from the Temple elms,
And at my feet the pale green Thames
Lies like a rod of rippled jade.

*Oscar Wilde*

## Sounds in the Wind

I can hear in the wind

a wandering werewolf,
howling, hunting, haunting,

321

a jumbling giant,
barging, bashing, breaking,

a dare-devil dragon,
racing, roaming, roaring,

a bruising bully,
pinching, punching, pushing,

a vicious vampire,
teasing, taunting, torturing,

a merciless monster,
smashing, slashing, storming.

I can hear the clouds being swept away
like mud from a clear, blue lake.

*Kate Williams*

## King Charles II

Here lies our mutton-eating King
Whose word no man relies on,
Who never said a foolish thing,
Nor ever did a wise one.

*John Wilmot, Earl of Rochester*

322

## Morning after a Storm

There was a roaring in the wind all night;
The rain came heavily and fell in floods;
But now the sun is rising calm and bright;
The birds are singing in the distant woods;
Over his own sweet voice the stock-dove broods;
The Jay makes answer as the Magpie chatters;
And all the air is filled with pleasant noise of waters.

All things that love the sun are out of doors;
The sky rejoices in the morning's birth;
The grass is bright with rain-drops – on the moors
The hare is running races in her mirth;
And with her feet she from the plashy earth
Raises a mist, that, glittering in the sun,
Runs with her all the way, wherever she doth run.

*from* Resolution and Independence
*William Wordsworth*

## What Went Wrong at My Sister's Wedding

The bridegroom was supposed
To kiss the bride,
Not kick 'er

And

He shouldn't have kissed
The Vicar

*And*

They should have thrown
Confetti,
Not

Spaghetti.

*Kit Wright*

## Throughout the world

Throughout the world if it were sought,
  Fair words enough a man shall find;
They be good cheap, they cost right nought,
  Their substance is but only wind.
But well to say and so to mean,
That sweet accord is seldom seen.

*Sir Thomas Wyatt*

# *X is for . . .*

# If words confuse
### An ode to the joyfulness of the rhythm of words

If words confuse
Then let us use
The language of the girls and boys
Far, far away
And everyday
Let's shout them out and feel their noise

'Tis great the sound
Our words abound
To celebrate the utter joys
How does it feel
To now reveal
Their truth and their feel joyous noise

These words laid
These phrases made
To captivate with style and poise
Forever roll
Enchant the soul
When we join and feel their noise.

*Neville Ambrose Xavier*

# Y is for . . .

## Had I the Heavens' Embroidered Cloths . . .

Had I the heavens' embroidered cloths,
Enwrought with golden and silver light,
The blue and the dim and the dark cloths
Of night and light and the half-light;
I would spread the cloths under your feet:
But I, being poor, have only my dreams;
I have spread my dreams under your feet;
Tread softly because you tread on my dreams.

                                    *W. B. Yeats*


## Very Famous Feet

My very famous feet
Are walking down the street
    Goal-scorers
    Crowd-pleasers
My very famous feet

My very famous feet
Strangers to defeat
    Penalty-takers
    Boot-wearers
My very famous feet

331

My very famous feet
In trainers looking neat
   Ball-dribblers
   Cup-winners
My very famous feet

My very famous feet
Are rushing through the gate
   Playground-pounders
   Classroom-visitors
My very famous feet

My very famous
   Very famous
My 'Sorry I'm late, Miss' feet

*Bernard Young*

*Z is for . . .*

## *People Need People*

To walk to
To talk to
To cry and rely on,
People will always need people.
To love and to miss
To hug and to kiss,
It's useful to have other people.
To whom will you moan
If you're all alone,
It's so hard to share
When no one is there,
There's not much to do
When there's no one but you,
People will always need people.

To please
To tease
To put you at ease,
People will always need people.
To make life appealing
And give life some meaning,
It's useful to have other people.
If you need a change
To whom will you turn,
If you need a lesson
From whom will you learn,
If you need to play
You'll know why I say
People will always need people.

As girlfriends,
As boyfriends,
From Bombay
To Ostend,
People will always need people.
To have friendly fights with
And share tasty bites with,
It's useful to have other people.
People live in families
Gangs, posses and packs,
It seems we need company
Before we relax,
So stop making enemies
And let's face the facts,
People will always need people,
Yes
People will always need people.

*Benjamin Zephaniah*

## *Celebration*

is daring
to be
who we are
it's like dancing
on table tops
while the world spins
and the fear stops
and the waves crash
and the stars glow
and the heart beats
and inside your head
you hear this song
rising
up
like laughter
rising
up
like a firework
soaring and weightless
to fill the whole sky
with joy

*Ann Ziety*

## *People*

Some people talk and talk
and never say a thing.
Some people look at you
and birds begin to sing.

Some people laugh and laugh
and yet you want to cry.
Some people touch your hand
and music fills the sky.

*Charlotte Zolotow*

# Index of First Lines

# Index of Poets

# Acknowledgements

The compiler and publishers would like to thank the following for permission to reprint the selections in this book:

**John Agard**, 'The Older the Violin the Sweeter the Tune' copyright © John Agard 1986, by permission of Caroline Sheldon Literary Agency Limited on behalf of the author; **Allan Ahlberg**, 'Friendly Matches' from *Friendly Matches* by Allan Ahlberg, Viking (2001), copyright © Allan Ahlberg 2001, by permission of Penguin Books Ltd; **Moira Andrew**, 'Portrait of a Dragon', first published in *Dragon Poems*, ed. John Foster, OUP (1991), by permission of the author; **Maya Angelou**, 'Life Doesn't Frighten Me' from *And Still I Rise* by Maya Angelou, Virago (1978), copyright © 1978 Maya Angelou, by permission of Time Warner Books UK; **Simon Armitage**, 'The Catch' from *Kid* by Simon Armitage (2002), by permission of Faber and Faber Ltd; **W. H. Auden**, 'Night Mail' from *Collected Poems* by W. H. Auden (1991), by permission of Faber and Faber Ltd; **Pam Ayres**, 'Oh, I Wish I'd Looked After Me Teeth' from *The Works* by Pam Ayres, BBC Books, copyright © Pam Ayres 1992, by permission of Sheil Land Associates Ltd on behalf of the author; **David Bateman**, 'The Feeling of Snow Before the Snow Itself Falls', by permission of the author; **Hilaire Belloc**, 'The Vulture', by permission of PFD on behalf of the estate of the author; **Catherine Benson**, 'Early to Bed Early to Rise', by permission of the author; **Clare Bevan**, 'Todd the Backyard King', by permission of the author; **Malorie Blackman**, 'Facing the Truth – with Haikus' from *Cloud Busting* by Malorie Blackman, Doubleday (2004), by permission of the Random House Group Ltd; **Valerie Bloom**, 'Neighbours', first printed in *Hot Like Fire*, Bloomsbury Children's Books, by permission of the author; **Gary Boswell**, 'School Sports Day Confession', by permission of the author; **Tony Bradman**, 'Ten Slightly Unfamiliar Sayings', first published in *Very Silly Lists*, Penguin Books Ltd, copyright © Tony Bradman 2000, by permission of The Agency (London) Ltd; **Redvers Brandling**, 'When did I get worse?', by permission of the author; **Alan Brownjohn**, 'Saturday Morning Where I Live', by permission of the author; **Liz Brownlee**, 'Jungle Jive', by permission of the author; **Dave Calder**, 'This is not an apple', by permission of the author; **Richard Caley**, 'Close to the Smiles of a Million Children', by permission of the author; **James Carter**, 'Road', copyright © James Carter 2006, by permission of the author; **Charles Causley**, 'Freddie Phipps' from *Collected Poems*, Macmillan, by permission of David Higham Associates on behalf of the author; **Debjani Chatterjee**, 'Let Sleeping Dogs Lie', by permission of the author; **Mandy Coe**, 'The Strawberry-yogurt Smell of Words', by permission of the author; **John Coldwell**, 'The Diary Of The Girl We All Want To Sit Next To When Her Best Friend Is

# Acknowledgements

Absent', by permission of the author; **Billy Collins**, 'On Turning Ten' from *Taking Off Emily Dickinson's Clothes* by Billy Collins, copyright © Billy Collins, by permission of SLL/Sterling Lord Literistic, Inc; **Pie Corbett**, 'A Chance in France', first printed in *Rice, Pie and Moses*, Macmillan Children's Books, by permission of the author; **June Crebbin**, 'The Whistler', by permission of the author; **e. e. cummings**, 'maggie and milly and molly and may' from *Complete Poems 1904–1962* by e. e. cummings, ed. George J. Firmage, copyright © 1991 by the Trustees for the E E Cummings Trust and George James Firmage, by permission of W. W. Norton & Company; **Jennifer Curry**, 'Pickety Witch', by permission of the author; **Roald Dahl**, 'I've Eaten Many Strange and Scrumptious Dishes' from *James and the Giant Peach* by Roald Dahl, Penguin, by permission of David Higham Associates on behalf of the estate of the author; **Jan Dean**, 'Nativity', first published in *Wallpapering the Cat*, Macmillan Children's Books (2003), by permission of the author; **Walter de la Mare**, 'The Scarecrow' from *The Complete Poems of Walter de la Mare* (1969), by permission of the Society of Authors on behalf of the literary trustees of Walter de la Mare and the Society of Authors as their representative; **Graham Denton**, 'Bending . . . the Truth', by permission of the author; **John C. Desmond**, 'We All Have To Go', by permission of the author; **Peter Dixon**, 'Missing Important Things', by permission of the author; **Gina Douthwaite**, 'Beware the Bush', by permission of the author; **Carol Ann Duffy**, 'The Famous' from *The Oldest Girl in the World* by Carol Ann Duffy, by permission of the author; **Helen Dunmore**, 'playground haiku' from *Snollygoster and Other Poems* by Helen Dunmore, Scholastic Children's Books (2001), by permission of A. P. Watt Ltd on behalf of the author; **Sue Dymoke**, 'Hiding Places', first published in *I Remember, I Remember*, Macmillan Children's Books (2003), by permission of the author; **George Marriott Edgar**, 'The Lion and Albert', copyright © George Marriott Edgar 1933, by permission of Francis Day & Hunter Ltd, London WC2H 0QY; **Richard Edwards**, 'Some Favourite Words', by permission of the author; **T. S. Eliot**, 'Macavity: The Mystery Cat' from *Old Possum's Book of Practical Cats* by T. S. Eliot (1982), by permission of Faber and Faber Ltd; **U. A. Fanthorpe**, 'What the Donkey Saw' from *Christmas Poems*, U. A. Fanthorpe (2002), by permission of Peterloo Poets and Enitharmon; **Eleanor Farjeon**, 'Books' from *Blackbird Has Spoken* by Eleanor Farjeon, Macmillan, by permission of David Higham Associates on behalf of the estate of the author; **Eric Finney**, 'Haiku Through the Year', by permission of the author; **John Foster**, 'I dream of a time', first published in *Standing on the Sidelines*, Oxford University Press (1995), by permission of the author; **Vivian French**, 'A Fishy Thought', by permission of the author; **Robert Frost**, 'Prayer in Spring' from *The Poetry of Robert Frost*, ed. Edward Connery Latham, Jonathan Cape, by permission of the Random House Group Ltd; **Roy Fuller**, 'Advice to Children', by permission of John Fuller; **Pam Gidney**, 'The Ancient Wizard's Daughter', by permission of the

# Acknowledgements

author; **Mick Gowar**, 'Boots', by permission of the author; **Harry Graham**, 'Presence of Mind', by permission of Laura Dance; **Robert Graves**, 'The *Alice Jean*' from *Graves' Complete Poems in One*, by permission of Carcanet Press Ltd; **Sophie Hannah**, 'The World is a Box', first published in *The Box Room* by Sophie Hannah, Orchard Books (2001), by permission of the author; **David Harmer**, 'A Story of Snowballs', by permission of the author; **Michael Harrison**, 'Haircut' from *Junk Mail*, Oxford University Press (1993), by permission of the author; **Seamus Heaney**, 'The Railway Children' from *Station Island* by Seamus Heaney (1984), by permission of Faber and Faber Ltd; **Stewart Henderson**, 'Through another day', first published in *All Things Weird and Wonderful* by Steward Henderson, Lion Children's Books (2003), by permission of the author; **Diana Hendry**, 'The Cullen Skink', by permission of the author; **Adrian Henri**, 'The Dark' from *Rhinestone Rhino* by Adrian Henri, Egmont, copyright © Adrian Henri 1989, by permission of Rogers, Coleridge & White Ltd on behalf of the author; **Phoebe Hesketh**, 'Sally' from *The Leave Train: New and Selected Poems* by Phoebe Hesketh (1994), by permission of Enitharmon Press; **Russell Hoban**, 'Homework' from *Egg Thoughts and Other Frances Songs*, Faber and Faber Ltd, by permission of David Higham Associates on behalf of the author; **Mary Ann Hoberman**, "Brother' from *The Llama Who Had No Pajama* by Mary Ann Hoberman (1998), copyright © Mary Ann Hoberman 1998, by permission of Gina Maccoby Literary Agency on behalf of the author; **A. E. Housman**, 'The Elephant', by permission of the Society of Authors as the literary representative of the estate of A. E. Housman; **Libby Houston**, 'The Trees Dance', first published in *All Change* by Libby Houston, Oxford University Press (1993), by permission of the author; **Langston Hughes**, 'Final Curve' from *Collected Poems of Langston Hughes*, Alfred A. Knopf Inc., by permission of David Higham Associates on behalf of the estate of the author; **Ted Hughes**, 'The Harvest Moon' from *Season Songs* by Ted Hughes, by permission of Faber and Faber Ltd; **Robert Hull**, 'Houses', by permission of the author; **Lucinda Jacob**, 'The Dream of the Plastic Bag', by permission of the author; **Huw James**, 'Fighting the Tide', by permission of the author; **Elizabeth Jennings**, 'The Black Cat's Conversation' from *A Spell of Words* by Elizabeth Jennings, Macmillan, by permission of David Higham Associates on behalf of the author; **Mike Johnson**, 'Solo Flight', by permission of the author; **Brian Jones**, 'About Friends' from *Spitfire on the Northern Line* by Brian Jones, Chatto & Windus (1975), by permission of The Random House Group Ltd; **Jenny Joseph**, 'Towards the End of Summer' was included in *All the Things I See* by Jenny Joseph, Macmillan Children's Books (2000), by permission of the author; **Jackie Kay**, 'An Old Woman's Fire', by permission of the author; **Penny Kent**, 'The ways of words', by permission of the author; **Jean Kenward**, 'Apple Crumble', by permission of the author; **Dick King-Smith**, 'Look Back in Wonder', by permission of A. P. Watt Ltd on behalf of the author; **Daphne Kitching**, 'Come Camping', first published in *Are*

# Acknowledgements

*We Nearly There Yet?*, ed. Brian Moses, Macmillan Children's Books (2002), by permission of the author; **John Kitching**, 'Really Really', by permission of the author; **Stephen Knight**, 'The Final Kick', first published in *Sardines*, Young Picador (2004), by permission of the author; **Naoshi Koriyama**, 'Unfolding Bud' from the July 3 (1957) issue of the *Christian Science Monitor*, copyright © 1957 the Christian Science Monitor, by permission of the Christian Science Monitor; **Tony Langham**, 'Taking Care of Business', by permission of the author; **Philip Larkin**, 'Take One Home for the Kiddies' from *Collected Poems* by Philip Larkin, by permission of Faber and Faber Ltd; **Ian Larmont**, 'Family Doctor', first published in *Fiendishly Funny Poems*, ed. John Foster, HarperCollins, by permission of the author; **C. S. Lewis**, 'The Dragon Speaks', copyright © C. S. Lewis Pte Ltd 1994, by permission of the C. S. Lewis Company Ltd; **Dorothy Livesay**, 'And Even Now' from *Archive for Our Time*, Dorothy Livesay, ed. Dean Irvine, by permission of Arsenal Pulp Press, Vancouver; **Liz Lochhead**, 'Poem For My Sister', by permission of Polygon, an imprint of Birlinn Ltd; **Tony Lucas**, 'By the Lake', by permission of the author; **Kevin McCann**, 'The Sea', first published in *Poems to take on Holiday*, ed. Susie Gibbs, Oxford University Press (2004), by permission of the author; **Roger McGough**, 'Wouldn't It Be Funny If You Didn't Have a Nose?', by permission of the author; **Lindsay MacRae**, 'Why Old People Say the Things They Do When Young People Ask Them How They Are', first published in *How to Make a Snail Fall in Love with You*, Puffin (2003), by permission of the author; **Wes Magee**, 'When the Funfair Comes to Town', by permission of the author; **Margaret Mahy**, 'Cat in the Dark', by permission of Watson, Little Ltd on behalf of the author; **John Masefield**, 'Sea Fever', by permission of the Society of Authors as the literary representative of the estate of John Masefield; **Gerda Mayer**, 'Fragment', first published in *Ariel* magazine 1971, by permission of the author; **Eve Merriam**, 'Giving Thanks Giving Thanks' from *Fresh Paint* by Eve Merriam, copyright © Eve Merriam 1986, by permission of Marian Reiner on behalf of the author; **Spike Milligan**, 'Onamatapia', by permission of Spike Milligan Productions Ltd; **Trevor Millum**, 'I like to swing on my own', by permission of the author; **Adrian Mitchell**, 'Ode To My Nose' from *Balloon Lagoon*, Adrian Mitchell, Orchard Books, copyright © Adrian Mitchell 1997, by permission of PFD on behalf of the author; **Tony Mitton**, 'Plum', first printed in *Plum*, Scholastic (1998), by permission of the author; **John Mole**, 'Another Day on the Beach', by permission of the author; **Edwin Morgan**, 'The Loch Ness Monster's Song' from *Collected Poems* by Edwin Morgan (1990), by permission of Carcanet Press Ltd; **Michaela Morgan**, 'A to Z', by permission of the author; **Brian Moses**, 'Our Ditch', first published in *Taking Out the Tigers* by Brian Moses, Macmillan Children's Books, by permission of the author; **Andrew Motion**, 'In the Attic' from *The Pleasure Steamers* by Andrew Motion, Carcanet (1978), by permission of PFD on behalf of the author; **Frances Nagle**, 'Year 6 Residential', first published in *Beware the Dinner Lady*, Macmillan Children's Books, by permission of the author; **Ogden Nash**, 'The Hippopotamus' from *Candy Is Dandy: The Best of Ogden Nash*, ed. Anthony Burgess, Andre Deutsch, copyright © Ogden Nash, by permission of Carlton Publishing Group; **Judith Nicholls**, 'The Door', by permission of the author; **Alfred Noyes**, 'The Moon Is Up', by permission of the Society of Authors as the literary representative of the estate of Alfred Noyes; **David Orme**, 'Incy Wincy', by permission of the author; **Jack Ousbey**, 'Gran Can You Rap?', first published in *All the Family*, ed. John Foster, Oxford University Press (1993), by permission of the author; **Gareth Owen**, 'Jemima', by permission of the author; **Brian Patten**, 'Reading the Classics', first published in *Juggling with Gerbils*, Puffin Books (2000), by permission of the author c/o Rogers, Coleridge and White; **Mervyn Peake**, 'Some Aunts and Uncles' from *A Book of Nonsense* by Mervyn Peake, Peter Owen Books, by permission of David Higham Associates on behalf of the estate of the author; **Andrew Fusek Peters**, 'Last Night I Saw the City Breathing', first broadcast on *Wham Bam Strawberry Jam*, BBC (1996), by permission of the author; **Polly Peters**, 'Cousin Autumn', first published in *Poems About Seasons*, ed. Andrew Fusek Peters, Hodder Wayland (2000), by permission of the author; **Gervase Phinn**, 'The Way I Am', by permission of the author; **Simon Pitt**, 'Marshmallow', by permission of the author; **Sylvia Plath**, extract from *The Bed Book* by Sylvia Plath, by permission of Faber and Faber Ltd; **Alan Priestley**, 'Worms Make Me Squirm', by permission of the author; **Janis Priestley**, 'But Of Course There Was Nobody There', by permission of the author; **Irene Rawnsley**, 'Darling Andrea' from *House of a Hundred Cats*, Methuen Children's Books (1995), by permission of the author; **Rita Ray**, 'Bouncy Castle', by permission of the author; **James Reeves**, 'Spells' from *Complete Poems for Children* by James Reeves, copyright © James Reeves Estate, by permission of Laura Cecil Literary Agency on behalf of the estate of the author; **John Rice**, 'Careful With That, You Might Break It', by permission of the author; **Chris Riley**, 'When I Came Home on Tuesday', previously published as 'Shrove Tuesday' in *Festivals*, ed. Jill Bennett, Scholastic (1994), by permission of the author; **Theodore Roethke**, 'The Sloth' from *Collected Poems* by Theodore Roethke, by permission of Faber and Faber Ltd; **Michael Rosen**, 'For Naomi' from *You wait till I'm older than you!* by Michael Rosen, Viking Penguin (1996), copyright © Michael Rosen 1996, by permission of PFD on behalf of the author; **Coral Rumble**, 'Seasoned Cinquains', first published in *Frogs in Clogs*, ed. Gaby Morgan, Macmillan Children's Books, by permission of the author; **Anita Marie Sackett**, 'Riddle', by permission of the author; **Carl Sandburg**, 'Who Do You Think You Are?'; extract from #64 in *The People, Yes* by Carl Sandburg, copyright © 1936 Harcourt, Inc., renewed 1964 by Carl Sandburg, by permission of Harcourt, Inc.; **Siegfried Sassoon**, 'Everyone Sang', by permission of Barbara Levy Literary Agency on behalf of the estate of the author; **Vernon Scannell**, 'The Apple Raid',

# Acknowledgements

by permission of the author; **Andrea Shavick**, 'How to Successfully Persuade Your Parents to Give You More Pocket Money', first published in *Unzip Your Lips Again*, ed. Paul Cookson, Macmillan Children's Books, by permission of the author; **Matt Simpson**, 'Nature's Paintbox', by permission of the author; **Ian Souter**, 'My Dad's Amazing!', by permission of the author; **Roger Stevens**, 'Chalk', first published in *The Monster That Ate the Universe*, Macmillan Children's Books, by permission of the author: **Marian Swinger**, 'Cracks in the Pavement', by permission of the author; **Dylan Thomas**, 'The Song of the Mischievous Dog', by permission of David Higham Associates on behalf of the estate of the author; **Nick Toczek**, 'Dragons Are Back', first published in *Dragons!*, Macmillan Children's Books (2005), by permission of the author; **J. R. R. Tolkien**, 'The Cat' from *The Adventures of Tom Bombadil* by J. R. R. Tolkien (1962), by permission of HarperCollins Publishers Ltd; **Angela Topping**, 'The New Generation', by permission of the author; **Jill Townsend**, 'Fox Shopping', by permission of the author; **John Turner**, 'Batman', by permission of the author; **Steve Turner**, 'In My Day', first published in *The Day I Fell Down the Toilet*, Lion (1996), by permission of the author; **Kaye Umansky**, 'An Alien Ate My Homework', by permission of the author; **Judith Viorst**, 'Harvey' from *If I Were in Charge of the World and Other Worries* by Judith Viorst, by permission of Lescher & Lescher Ltd on behalf of the author; **Jaroslav Vrchlicky**, 'For a Little Love', included in *Sheep Don't Go to School*, ed. Andrew Fusek Peters, tr. Andrew and Vera Fusek Peters, Bloodaxe Books (1999), by permission of Andrew Fusek Peters; **Philip Waddell**, 'The Story of My Life – List of Discontents', by permission of the author; **Barrie Wade**, 'My Old Bear', by permission of the author; **Celia Warren**, 'Pelican', by permission of the author; **Clive Webster**, 'An Old Plot of Land', by permission of the author; **Colin West**, 'Some Stuff in a Sack', by permission of the author; **John Whitworth**, 'The Vikings', by permission of the author; **Ian Whybrow**, 'Last Steam Train to Moorgate', by permission of the author; **Kate Williams**, 'Sounds in the Wind', by permission of the author; **Kit Wright**, 'What Went Wrong at My Sister's Wedding', by permission of the author; **W. B. Yeats**, 'He Wishes For the Cloths of Heaven', by permission of A. P. Watt Ltd on behalf of Michael B. Yeats; **Bernard Young**, 'Very Famous Feet', by permission of the author; **Benjamin Zephaniah**, 'People Need People' from *Wicked World* by Benjamin Zephaniah, copyright © Benjamin Zephaniah 2000, by permission of PFD on behalf of the author; **Charlotte Zolotow**, 'People' from *All That Sunlight* by Charlotte Zolotow, copyright © 1967, renewed 1995 by Charlotte Zolotow, by permission of Scott Treimel NY on behalf of the author.

Every effort has been made to trace the copyright holders, but if any have been inadvertently overlooked the publishers will be pleased to make the necessary arrangement at the first opportunity.